Ten Fundamentals for Durable Peace and Prosperity in the African Great Lakes Region
(Rwanda, Burundi, Uganda, DRC)

Understanding the True Role of the United States of America, the Belgium, the France, and the United Kingdom

VOLUME II
Positive Change of Negative Mentality
English Version

Br. Paterne Muhaya Bengehya

With Preface of
Thomas D. McFarland, PhD.
Illustrated by Paulin Engambe

2

Contents

Acronyms and Abbreviations   4

Chapter Seven
Positive Change of Negative Mentality   6

7.1. Acquisition of New Minds: A Necessity for
Durable Peace and Prosperity for all in the   6
AGLR

7.2. Some Negative Mentalities that should
Change for the Sake of Durable Peace and   14
Prosperity for All
      7.2.1. Slave Mentality (SM)   14
      7.2.2. Victim Mentality (VM)   50
      7.2.3. African Colonization Mentality   69
      (ACM)
      7.2.4. Black African Racism Mentality
      (BARM) – Black Africans against   89
      Africans
      7.2.5. Witchcraft or Sorcery Mentality   123
      (WSM)
      7.2.6. Natural Resources   149
      Mismanagement Mentality (NRMM)
      7.2.7. Chronic Laziness and Easy Life   239
      Mentality (CLELM)
      7.2.8. Time Mismanagement Mentality   247
      (TMM)

      7.2.9. Harmful African Traditional   316
      Mentality (HATM)

7.2.10. Gender Imbalance Mentality (GIM)   327

References   **383**

Acronyms and Abbreviations

ACM: African Colonization Mentality
AFRUCA: Africans United Against Child Abuse
AGLR: African Great Lakes Region
AGLR: African Great Lakes Region
BARM: Black African Racism Mentality
CEDAW: Convention on the Elimination of All Forms of
       Discrimination Against Women
CLELM: Chronic Laziness and Easy Life Mentality
DRC: Democratic Republic of Congo
FAO: Food and Agriculture Organization
GIM: Gender Imbalance Mentality
HATM: Harmful African Traditional Mentality
ICTR: International Criminal Tribunal for Rwanda
IUCN: International Union for Conservation of Nature
MFPED: Ugandan Ministry of Finance, Planning and
       Economic Development
MGLSD: Ministry of Gender, Labor and Social
       Development
MONUSCO: The United Nations Organization
       Stabilization Mission in the Democratic Republic
       of the Congo
ND: No Date
NRMM: Natural Resources Mismanagement Mentality
OSESG-GL: Office of the Special Envoy for the Great
       Lakes
SM: Slave Mentality
TMM: Time Mismanagement Mentality
UDHR: Universal Declaration of Human Rights
UK: United Kingdom

UNDP: United Nations Development Program
UNEP: United Nation Environment Program
USD: United States Dollar
USIP: United States Institute of Peace
VM: Victim Mentality
WSM: Witchcraft or Sorcery Mentality

Chapter Seven
Positive Change of Negative Mentality

"Don't live the same day over and over again and call that a life. Life is about evolving mentally, spiritually, and emotionally." (Germany Kent).

7.1. Acquisition of New Minds: A Necessity for Durable Peace and Prosperity for all in the AGLR

The people of AGLR in need of peace have to acknowledge that there is a crucial need of change of mentality on a number of facts that have direct links and impacts on everyday life in the region. People need positive change of mindsets that will result in positive attitude of minds that are ready to welcome principles that build durable peace and prosperity for all by destroying those which demolish it.

Positive Change of Mentality is not something that can easily be done; it requires the self-examination of conscious and serious personal decisions that will be followed by the acquisition of new mindsets. We all need new minds if we want to live news lives of full peace and prosperity. "We can't solve problems by using the same kind of thinking we used when we created them." (Albert Einstein). People need to accept change although it is sometimes shocking or unpleasant because we cannot solve our problems with the minds that created them.

Positive Change Mentality is very necessary because of its impacts on human minds where people's happiness and sadness dwell. When people choose negative change, they follow the path of misery and sadness; when they choose positive change, they welcome joy, security, stability, harmony, respect, self-discovery, self-reliance, etc. which are the symptoms of peace and prosperity. That is why new minds for the populations of the African Great Lakes Region are necessary for their good future.

In his book 'Five Minds for the Future', Gardner (2006) talks about the disciplined mind, the synthesizing mind, the creative mind, the respect mind, and the ethical mind. The disciplined mind will help people to work steadily over time in order to improve skill and understanding. It can be agreed that people need skills and understandings to be able to produce – production being crucial for durable peace and prosperity for all – things that they really need to live a peaceful and prosperous life. The synthesizing mind, as explained by Gardner, is really needed in this developing world crowded by many and various information. This mind will help people to take information from disparate sources, to understand and evaluate it objectively, and to put it together in ways that make sense to the synthesizer and also to other persons. I assume that this mind capacity is more needed in the AGLR more than it is in other regions of the world. A region full of diverse and conflict bearing information need leaders and even followers with the capacity to synthesize and analyze locally what they hear and read.

The creating new minds will help people to produce new ideas, to pose unfamiliar questions, to conjure up fresh ways of thinking resulting in finding unexpected answers to seemingly difficult questions. The AGLR, as it is known, has many and challenges that seem impossible and difficult to be successfully overcome. Can this region of African be self-reliant one day although its rich natural potential? Can people of this region be able to suppress the barriers to their harmonious interpersonal and intercultural communication? Will it have good leaders in the future? Can its general populations access the 'true truth' about themselves and their lands instead of relying no the lies of some of their fake leaders? Is positive change of mentality possible for the average citizens of the countries of the AGLR? Is really durable peace and prosperity for all possible, or it is a non-achievable dream?

When people possess the disciplined and synthesizing minds, they can avoid so many events or problems that could destroy their well-being. I strongly believe that when people change, the reality of their lives changes too. But everybody will not change the same way as others even all of them have changed positively for the good of the whole community.

That is why the respectful mind suggested by Gardner is also needed. It recognizes and accepts the differences between human beings and between human groups like political parties, ethnic groups, nationalities, etc. with the aim of effectively working with them. We need to agree with the fact that there are inevitable social links between the human individuals regardless their identities; that is why tolerance and respect are primordial virtues in people's day to day interactions.

One of the strong reasons about that is the reality that we exist to serve others in the community – to serve our gifts to the world where we live – after discovering the needs of the people. With this knowledge, Gardner's fifth suggested mind for the future 'the ethical mind' looked at. It stresses on the nature of one's work and the needs and desires of the society in which one lives. It helps workers to serve the purposes beyond their self-interests and the citizens to work unselfishly to improve the lot of all (Gardner, 2006).

To my humble opinion, all the populations of the AGLR regardless their country of origin needs the five minds for the future suggested by Gardner. If these are some of the minds that people need, what are some of the minds that need changes for a better future of durable peace and prosperity for all? What negative mentalities that exist in the AGLR and need to be changed into positive ones?

In fact, some of the main points on which most Africans need to accept change of mentality are the following: slave mentality, colonialist mentality, victim mentality, black Africans colonization mentality, racism and discriminative mentality (egoism, tribalism, ethnics, and regionalism), witchcraft and wizards mentality, resources-waste mentality (mismanagement), easy-life dream mentality (expecting aid, Ubuntu that renders null and void, laziness, pretending behavior – especially for some educated people thinking high of themselves by neglecting some jobs -, and carelessness), time mismanagement mentality, gender discrimination mentality (discrimination of women, overestimation of man, family violence, man as a king in the family), and gossip and too much talking mentality.

7.2. Some Negative Mentalities that should Change for the Sake of Durable Peace and Prosperity

7.2.1. Slave Mentality (SM)

"Emancipate yourselves from mental slavery, none but ourselves can free our minds!"
(Marcus Garvey)

What is Slave Mentality?

The slave mentality is a situation in which people limit themselves psychologically by accepting to be under influence or domination of someone else or something else; it makes people live in detrimental conditions by limiting their beliefs and inner freedom. So, people willing to live in peace and prosperity will not accept to be enslaved in any manner. They will make strides to liberate themselves from the 'slave mentality' and will develop a high self-confidence. They will make sure there are living independent lives. People free from slave mentality are original in their thoughts, their beliefs, their behaviors, their speeches, their acts. They enjoy the freedom of being 'themselves' and using their true inborn capacities to live free and happy lives.

The mentality that pushes African people to live like slaves is one of the negative impacts of slavery on Africa continent; it is also the result of the acts of some fake political leaders and the teachings of some religious leaders. This mentality kills people's effort to discover and use their true selves and to develop their natural abilities which are important to personal success (prosperity) and peace. The following statements can be considered as symptoms of slave mentality in the AGLR. In other words, people with slave mentality tend to have some of the following opinions.

- Only the white man can do that!

- Africans are not smart enough to lead Africa to durable peace and prosperity for all.

- It's okay; we have always been living like that.

- That is how the situation has always been; we have nothing to do.

- Our ancestors have tried and failed; I am not the one who can succeed!

- The situation cannot change; we will always be under their influence.

- Don't even try nothing will change.

- I am in need of assistance because even if I try, I cannot solve my problems.

- I was created to be working for him/her; there is no need for me to complain about what he/she is doing against me.

- My troops cannot fight like the neighbors; they are naturally fit for war than us.

- I cannot waste my time thinking about what I did not create; it's not my responsibility.

- I am not able to do anything to prosper again; I am just waiting to die!

- Black Africans are bound to live a miserable life as the colonialists told our parents.

- It is not a problem even if I die poor and miserable because of my religion!

- It is not a problem even if I kill a non-believer; it is not a sin according to the teachings of my religion. I strongly believe that is true.

- It is not my responsibility to vote for leaders in my country; others will vote.

- African leaders cannot solve their problems themselves; I don't want to waste my time discussing about issues concerning durable peace and prosperity for all. I am just waiting to finish my mandate and rest.

- People of other religions cannot think and acts like us; we are the only people that God talk to. We are the only religion that conveys the true information about eternal life and happy life on earth.

- Our prophets/priests/pastors are the only ones to whom the true God speak to; we are the only church or religion that have true teachings and prophecies.

- Etc.

The following drawing shows how some people of AGLR are enslaved mentality by their religious leaders. This kind of mental attitudes about prophets and pastors need to be replaced by critical thinking skills so that people may be mentally free to make good decisions that will not kill their peace.

The so-called Servants of God who claim to have revelations from God most of time end up by misleading people. They are robbers of peace and prosperity.

"Our contribution has to be given not only
for the liquidation of the colonial system but also
for the liquidation of ignorance, disease
and primitive forms of social organization."
(António Agostinho Neto).

Taking into consideration some of the symptoms of slave mentality in the AGLR, it may be necessary to try to reflect on the following questions. What mentality do I have at this present moment about my own life? I am mentally free or I am a slave? Can anyone be happy to be slave, or I am looking for possible means that can make me free?

What can hinder my decision or effort to become mentally free? What can I do to break the hindrances to my efforts and decisions to become a free human being? Is possible for me to evaluate my progress during my process of becoming a free person? Do I have a clear understanding of 'slave mentality', its characteristics, and its impacts on the lives of many people in Africa? What does 'slave mentality' means to me and how can it put me in bondage?

Impact of Slave Mentality on Many of the People of AGLR

Living for a couple of years in the AGLR with an observation of how people live regardless the country they live in although the views of the observers may differ, the results are so alarming for the majority of the populations of the region. Most people seem to be continually under slavery and their socio-economic lives are strongly affected their states of mind. Some are living in terrible poverty and fear of tomorrow; they are just begging to live (beggar mentality).

Some are enslaved by the teachings, ideas, and ideologies of their ethnic or tribal leaders; they cannot think and acts by themselves. Some are locked in the teachings of their religions that hinder their social progress because they are taught to only love the people with same religious beliefs. They live an unhappy life of hate and scarcity because of the limitations imposed to them by their sects or religions. Some other people of the region are living in total ignorance of their human rights; they are compelled to blindly submit the unjust socioeconomic structures of their avenues, zones, provinces, countries.

Almost all the population of the AGLR needs a certain level of liberation especially in the area of universal human rights that most of their leaders violate. And the fear that envelops the minds of people and stops them from claiming their rights is a form of manifested 'slave mentality'. So, the great impact of 'slave mentality' on the populations of the AGLR can be seen in people poverty due to refusal of advices and counseling, fear of tomorrow, total dependency and self-consolation, lethargy or inactivity, and blind imitations that fragile the lives of many.

As it is known, slave mentality produces some negative effects that can be sum up with the following words: repulsion, acceptance, adjustment, reluctance, dependence, etc. So, the people with slave mentality are likely to,

- ✓ feel like they are inferior to others;
- ✓ have no hope at all (hopelessness);
- ✓ be in bondage for are limited in thoughts or do that themselves;
- ✓ depend totally on others to live (no personal imitative at all);
- ✓ eternally wait for other people to give them freedom;

- ✓ have much doubt and suspicion of people who try to help them;

- ✓ hate or avoid the power and advantages that come with freedom;

- ✓ dislike new experiences, things or persons – they are comforted with familiarity and routine – to them;

- ✓ avoid thinking about new opportunities, possibilities, and change – their expectations are of the same old things they know or do – that can lead to durable peace and prosperity;

- ✓ loose true personal identity and self-esteem with consequence of being disposed or object to peer pressure and criticisms;

- ✓ be weakened to resist pressures and prefer the least efforts to survival (inappropriate continual existence);

- ✓ dwell on the events of the past as if past and present are supposed to always be the same.

  By the way, the slave mentality in the AGLR manifests mostly in the following realities on many people in the region.

- ✓ Their own mentality put them in Bandage

The mental slavery in the AGLR seems to be as outrageous as the historic transatlantic slave trade, but many people do not realize it. It has negative impacts on durable peace and prosperity of the region. The fact is that many people seem to ignore its signs or to consider them as normal and important to live well. The irony of the issue is that things that are putting people in bandage in Africa are the ones that are attracting much their attention; they spend too much energy, money, time, etc. on things that are uprooting them and that will never allow them to live prosperous lives that lead to durable peace. They are mentally in bandage and some of the sings of that are seen in the following points.

- ✓ **The boundaries of the African countries fixed by non-Africans**

It is known that the conference of Berlin in 1885 shared African continent among the European powers that were doing colonial businesses in Africa. That fact was that the European leaders present at that conference did not consider the issue of technical or tribal belonging of African peoples in order to fix the boundaries of their traditional territories or areas to transform them into the countries Africa has today.

It is clear that European powers present at the conference of Berlin sought their personal colonial interests in detriment of any other aspects that would result in the formation of countries with respect for the African kingdom of the postcolonial era with one or few traditional culture and language. That is why you can be a Congolese of the DRC and have some uncles or ants who are Angolans; you can be a Rwandan and have some relatives who are Burundians; you can be a Ugandan and have your parents or grand-parents who are Congolese. That is very normal due to what happen during the Conference of Berlin. We do not need to hate the people of the neighboring countries, they are our relatives.

We know that the some politicians of the AGLR have used the boundaries fixed by the European colonialists serve their egoistic purposes. They have created the feeling of hate and disgust in the minds of many citizens. This development to become very serious by creating 'mental bandages' that do not allow people to live well their neighbors; they have locked many people to themselves while they need others to live in durable peace and prosperity. It is time to unlock the 'boundary bandage' created by the enemies of peace and prosperity for all in Africa.

Africans' mindsets about foreigners should be cleared from any negative stereotypes or information that may impede the good cooperation and collaboration. The people of AGLR are just One people divided only by the interests of the colonialists – and what they have done continue to strongly impact the region – who had the strategy of dividing people in order to detrimentally reign over them. Knowing this reality, the mentality of hating people of the neighboring countries can be considered insanity; because it will help no one to reach durable peace and prosperity.

✓ The Imposed European Languages

When foreign languages are given more importance in the national settings of a country, the local or national languages are likely to be neglected or given less importance. While national languages are very primordial to make alive the culture of a nation by communicating its values, beliefs, and customs to the world, foreign languages can only be considered as important when interaction is needed with foreigners or when some of them are accepted as official languages that sometimes serve as vernacular languages.

So, the mentality of considering the languages imposed by colonialists as the 'languages of developed people' may push people to live as if they were in western countries while they are in the AGLR; it may push them to forget their true identities and cultures. They may be tempted to think that durable peace and prosperity concerns only the people who speak French, English, Portuguese, Spanish, and German. In the African Great Lakes Region as in the whole African continent, black Africans were forced to adopt the languages of colonialists and to neglect their local languages. One of the consequences of that situation was the modification of the worldview of the Africans at the time of colonization. That did not finish in the past because the opinions of millions of Africans today about themselves and the world are the result what the history of Africa teaches them. Their mentalities are not so different from the mentalities of their parents and grandparents who suffered the mental and physical colonization of Europeans.

There is no best or special culture, there is no special language; it is known that some languages like French and

English are spoken worldwide making them international languages, but that does not make them communicators of special cultures. We need to understand that the knowledge of languages cannot guarantee durable peace and prosperity for all in a nation.

As a matter of fact, people who learn languages in order to become special, civilized, and developed end up by becoming mentally slaves – for languages does not bring wisdom people need to prosper in peace – of the foreign dialects and cultures. They waste time looking for things they need in the foreign countries while they possess them in their countries. They create conflicts with other thinking that they are superior to anyone who does not speak the languages they speak. That kind of mentality needs to be abandoned otherwise it will maintain its victims in eternal bandage.

✓ **The Inherited Way of Clothing**

Parents and/or grandparents of black Africans who were forced to speak like their master colonialists could not limit the civilization requirement to only languages; they were also forced to wear clothes the same way their masters do. While this mentality couldn't have any negative impact on African populations if adapted to the cultures, means, and environment conditions of Africa, millions of Africans in the AGLR today are spending too much money buying clothes that put them in conditions that do not fit their cultures, means, and climates. This situation robs the peace and prosperity of many families in Africa. For example, a woman may buy a cloth that will cost the money her husband gets for a two-month work as salary!

Some people are buying very expansive clothes to look like 'civilized persons'; they may eat inadequate foods, they may sleep in very worse conditions, they may lack means of transportation, they may also lack money to pay the school fees... but you will see them wearing clothes that are too expensive because they need to look nice and civilized or developed! As a result, their families remain in long-lasting poverty that deteriorates the family peace, and ends up by making some of their family member hooligans, street children, robbers, or peace destroyers in the community. We need to address this issue seriously.

It is for personal re-education in order to change the mentality of clothing like people of different nations and cultures while having different means and climatic conditions. This attitude is another form of 'mental bandage' that need to be broken. It happens at personal level like many other mental bandages but has community and national impact by the reality that individuals live in communities with direct interaction with others. Some of the youth, for instance, are making effort to cloth like western TV Stars or movie stars. They spend much money and time to be like 'stars' in terms of cloth in order to feel 'okay'! Some may steal money from their families, some may use a huge amount of the money they worked for, and some may chose to be begging from relatives and friends to cloth 'well' as if clothing like 'others' is a priority in their lives!

✓ **The Imported Religions**

The imported and imposed religions to Africans did not allow them to think and live like themselves. Those religions have molded some Africans into different peoples with serious modification and for some suppression of their cultures. While some practices in some African cultures were supposed to be suppressed to better access the paths to durable peace and development, there has been a birth of some attitudes from religions that have put people into mental bandage.

That 'religious bandage' in the minds of millions of Africans – especially in the AGLR where people suffer most the consequences of that – is a hindrance to personal development and freedom of the spirit that are necessary for the use of the true discovered self which is among the principles for durable peace and prosperity of the AGLR as suggested in this book.

The imported religions to Africa are to be thought as the cause of lack of peace and prosperity for all in the AGLR. But these religions become a threat to peace when their leaders fail to truthfully teach the contents of their sacred books or the doctrinal teachings; they also become dangerous when their adepts misunderstand the contents of their sacred books or doctrinal teachings that were well taught by their religious leaders. Because this situation has become frequent in Africa when many people who took part in religious activities are illiterate or have low critical thinking capacity, there is always a creation of 'religious bandage' in the minds of millions that make them mentally slaves.

Some fail to live will with their neighbors because they don't share the same religious beliefs; some consider only brothers and sisters the members of their religions or sects and anyone else is considered as not worthy of assistance or respect as a human being; some tend to not take care or being interested of the political issues of their countries – for example, they refuse to vote – due to their minds set about election as a result of their religious beliefs; some spend much time praying for durable peace and prosperity and then do nothing to reach it – they are lazy and reluctant to work hard – thinking that beliefs are enough to live well; some are locked by religions that teach them that killing a person who does not worship with them is not bad at all!; to name just a few.

That is how the mentalities created by imported religions in Africa differ and lock people in hostage. They are in prison in their minds and cannot move to important steps in their lives as long as there is no positive change of mind regarding their own religious beliefs, the religious beliefs of others, and the human being as a sacred creature deserving care, assistance, and respect as a special creature of God regardless their religious belongings. In fact, anyone who has a religious belief in the AGLR needs to understand that durable peace and prosperity for all is not a religious activity; it is a human activity and every human being is supposed to live in peace with themselves and others even if they do not belong to a religion.

We need to think and look beyond our personal religious precepts if we want to achieve what we are supposed to do on the planet earth; we need to think and act like that if we want Africa to become the good dreams we have about it. So, the imported religions in Africa should not serve as means of dividing peoples or making them busy, they are supposed to be accepted as one of the ways of helping African to discover their true abilities and use them to unlock the chains that put them in bandage so that they may live a peaceful and prosperous lives in union and harmony.

✓ The Non-African Names (Western Names, Christian Names, Islamic Names)

'Name' is universally known as a term or work that is used to identify a person, a group of people, a thing, a place, a country, a continent, etc. Before we know humans and things by other qualifiers, we used their 'names' as the first elements of identification. That is why, with reference to the continent, we sometimes recognize or qualify names to be European, African, American, Asian, etc. With reference to countries, we can know names to be Rwandan, Ugandan, Congolese, etc.

Names are then meant to be used for identification – to show a person's true identity – and people are to be pride with their names as they should with their identities. However, because of the atrocities committed by colonialists and the influence of some imported religions in Africa, many African today continue to believe the ugly lies that the non-African names are special or honor and respect conveying. And that is another fact that cements the walls that mentally imprison some Africans up to date. In the AGLR, there is a tendency of forgetting the true African meaning behind the name; most parents are putting much consideration to non-African names which are mostly Western names, 'Christian-given' names, and Muslim names. African traditional culture reserves important meaning on names given to things and to peoples.

There is no need to deny that as what was happening before the arrival of European colonialists in Africa. In some African kingdom, for example, giving names to babies meant that they have become human beings. Fitzpatrick (2012, p.31) means the same by putting

"Naming among the Congolese also holds immense importance. Among the Kongo ethnic group for instance, a newborn was not regarded truly human until the bestowal of a name." Due to the colonial hegemony and to the imported religions in Africa, people are still under the influence the ideas of colonialism and imported religious beliefs that had killed the original identity of Africans.

The reality of the human life on planet earth is that it does not develop to durable peace and prosperity out of its original and true nature as it was meant to be by the creator. It can be argued that the African culture cannot be appropriate to westerners and the western culture will not be so to Africans. Also, Africans cannot live in Africa as if they were in Europe; they cannot also live in Europe as if they were in Africa. Even the environmental and climatic conditions of the two continents are eloquent to show that there are significant differences between them. That was one of the truths that the European colonialists did not want to respect because of their egoistic business interests. They lied to the colonized people that their traditional practices and cultures were worse; they forced them to adopt the European ones in order to have social respect and consideration, in order to be 'civilized'.

That is why many Africans abandoned their African naming system by adopting those of colonialists thinking was the best one even up today. By arguing this way, I am not against the non-African names or the Western names at all – for I myself have a Western Christian name (Paterne) – but these names should not be considered by Africans as having more meaning or being special than names taken from African cultures. A name is not special or superior because of its western or Christian origin; it not special because it belonged to person who died long ago and who was proclaimed 'saint' par a certain religion!

We need to be Africans that are bearing and loving our true African identities with African dreams in order to help Africa to achieve durable peace and prosperity for its peoples. So, the people of the AGLR should have the identities of the region by removing the myths that are behind the non-African names so that they may be more concerned about African names by creating more love for Africa peace and prosperity.

✓ **The European (or Western) Eating Habits (Abandoning African Eating Habits)**

Another thing that makes people blocked in their mental capacities in their day to day activities is the European Food or European Kitchen. This fact calls the attention of a particular group of individuals in the AGLR who kill their own freedom to enjoy locally produced foods or local

African kitchen because they consider it as being for primitive people, uncivilized ones. They strongly believe that eating the way westerners eat will make them modern and civilized people. This is a kind of mental colonization and does not allow people to appear original their eating habit. It is does not sound reasonable to think about persuading or advising Africans to only eat like Africans, but the fact that unreasonable imitations are like to be destoyers of peace and prosperity is something to consider when addressing this issue.

Some of the African people with European eating habits think they are highly developed and civilized than other Africans. For example, during the colonization, the Belgian colonialists taught the Rwandans, Burundian, and Congolese people to be using knives, spoons, and forks when eating; and because they were taught to be putting the folk on the left-hand, anyone who breaks this rule by putting it on the right-hand will be considered as uncivilized by the people who are still mentally colonized by European eating rules or habits on the dining table.

The point here is that even if Africans continue to use the type of foods and the feeding habits learned from Europeans colonialists, they are not supposed to consider them as the best ones. Our African kitchen or eating habits should not be despised by Africans. They save time, money, and convey our true identities as Africans. We need to be proud when we eat like Africans in order to help feed millions of Africans who starving to have food. If we cannot be happy when eating like Africans, how can we help millions of Africans to be able to feed themselves in African manner?

Moreover, some African people have shown clearly their negative mindsets that lock them mentally when they access a higher social status in Africa. These people regardless their level of education or schooling, once their financial situations allow them to go up the social ladder, they automatically abandon the way they were eating like Africans. The one of the consequences of that is the incapacity for their bodies to cope with the new food habit and the lack of adequate information related to nutrition; as a result, some end up by suffering from some diseases.

Oniang'o (2003, p. 336) writes about the health implications of modern feeding habits of African peoples by showing their consequences. He put that "Modern feeding habits have brought a number of life-threatening nutritional disorders to Africa. These include: obesity, hypertension, diabetes mellitus, cancer, and cardiovascular disorders." Is it okay to increase one's incomes with the aim of making life more and more enjoyable and end up by imprisoning the body by what one chooses to be eating?

Can people change the nature of someone or something they did not create? Can a person change their own nature by trying to eat as other people? This issue may seem to be of less importance for some people in Africa and elsewhere in the world, but looking deeply on it can shed light to help understand that durable peace and prosperity for Africans will require them to revise even some facts in their lives that seem to be neglected by many.

We need to consider positive change of the mentality of not imitating the non-African ways of eating; if we do not stop that, it will be for many as one of the ways of destroying their true identities. And when the identity is destroyed or darkened, the true peace and prosperity of the individuals is at odd. People of the AGLR need to understand this and teach it to each other; the countries of the region do not need to be spending too much to take care of people who are suffering because of their own negative mentality.

While durable peace and prosperity will result in the change of social status of many in a nation, we should know and let our friend know that we do not change our social status to change our natural identities. We are Africans and we shall remain Africans although some are trying to show the world that they are not people of Africa by what they are eating, saying, wearing, and doing. Most of the problems that some African people face in Africa are made more serious by their own mentalities. For example, African investor aiming to invest in food industry and who believes that European food and Kitchen are best and appropriate for everybody even Africans will not be likely to invest his money in African food industry, yet that is the domain where millions of people need to be fed! Human beings naturally tend to give priority to things or people they love the most even if they are not the neediest ones. It takes much courage and maturity to be able to give priority on things or persons who are the neediest even if they are the ones we love the most.

7.2.2. Victim Mentality (VM)

"If it's never our fault, we can't take responsibility for it. If we can't take responsibility for it, we'll always be its victim." (Richard Bach)

What is victim mentality?

Victim mentality is a state of mind in which people keep on blaming others for the past or present situations by not willing to be helpful to themselves even when there are opportunities, power, or means available; they keep on accusing others or divinity as a way of avoiding to take responsibility or action to change life conditions; they are mostly inactive and keep on taking into consideration the harmful or atrocious conditions or circumstances to which they have been subjected by others or by fate without doing anything at all.

Kets de Vries (2012, p.3) writes about the people with the victim syndrome by putting, "These are people who always complain about the 'bad things that happen' in their lives, due to circumstances beyond their control. Nothing feels right to them. Trouble follows them wherever they go." In the African Great Lakes Region, there is too much to say about the victim mentality. Millions of people are living in very worse conditions because of civil wars, genocides, insecurity, and mismanagement of their leaders. Those people have, at one time of their history, been victims of atrocious acts that make them lose the lives of their beloved, their riches, the parts of their bodies, and many other more important things to their lives.

However, some of the losses that occurred in the AGLR can be repaired – especially the material and psycho-social losses – and lives of people can even become better than before, but many people of the region have locked themselves with the 'victim mentality' that has killed their hopes, personal efforts, dignity, self-esteem, etc. They are in an unpleasant situation of life and constitute a threat to durable peace and prosperity all in their respective countries. However, some of the people with 'victim mentality' in the AGLR may be heard whisper the following sentences or statements showing the symptoms of their state of mind.

- ✓ It is the people of Tutsi ethnic group who made my life like this and I will never prosper anymore.

- ✓ I am handicapped because of the people of Hutu ethnic group and I can do nothing to get well.

- ✓ I am so desperate because of the loss of all the members of my family; nothing can be done for me to regain my happiness.

- ✓ The Rwandan people are the ones that made our country in total ruin and insecurity; we are not able to improve the situation.

- ✓ We lost our courage because of the Congolese who gave our enemies accommodations to hide from us; that is why we are living in fear of tomorrow and we shall not escape their future attacks on our country.

- ✓ The Ugandan rebel troops had invaded our province that it why we shall never be able to adequately exploit our natural resources by our own skills in peace.

- ✓ Some Burundians are always involved in the plunder of the DR Congo natural resources; that is our country will never be prosperous by its own riches.

- ✓ We are not able to change the situation that had been created by the European colonialists.

- ✓ I am too poor and illiterate because my parents were slaves.

- ✓ Our country suffers many problems today because of the colonialists and almost all the Western powers are just reinforcing the nonconstructive legacies of colonization to maintain their superiority over us; we cannot do anything to change that because they are so powerful than us as the colonialists were.

- ✓ Etc.

These are just some of the statements that may clearly show the symptoms of victim mentality in the AGLR. We need to address that with much emphasis because if the mentality of many does not change, the leaders may work hard to establish durable peace and prosperity for all but their efforts will be in vain. That is very important because leaders in general and especially political leaders cannot develop a country without the contribution of the entire population.

We can assume that all the leaders of a country are willing to work for its development. But, the reality is that, some do it nicely leading people to durable peace and prosperity and some others do it badly leading their followers to durable troubles and poverty. That is why among the population of a country, leaders should be the first ones to have free minds; they must not be slaves, otherwise they will end up by enslaving many of the citizens. That is all about development that should not be misuse or misunderstood.

Gabriel, O. C. J. B. (2014, p. 80) inscribes "Development is not a matter of infrastructure but of structure. The idea of this structure had been given by Karl Marx in his 'Theory of the State', he called it *Superstructure*. This superstructure should be a mental construct that brings together the being, situation, hopes and aspiration of a people into one piece of developmental formula. With the so-called western education left in its colonial schemes, African development is still west-bound and may not favor those whom it never considered when it was being constructed." This passage from Gabriel's article shown, as we are arguing, that the 'development' is all about the good mental attitudes of individuals. It is not just the good material things that are seen, but it is first and foremost the mentalities of people which compose the 'superstructure.' If the mentalities of many African people change positively, the African development will cease to be measured by the influence of colonial ideologies. And many African people will become totally free to work for durable peace and prosperity for all.

Some Characteristics of Victim Mentality in the AGLR

With too much suffering due to the colonialists' awful policies and acts, the civil wars, the genocides, and other forms of atrocious acts committed by some African leaders in the AGLR, many people had lost things or individual beings of great importance to them. That resulted in serious psycho-social problems among with the 'victim mentality' that is one of the hindrances to their well-beings. The Victim Mentality (VM) syndromes manifest itself in the populations of the AGLR by the following characteristics.

- ✓ **People with VM ignore that they are barriers to their own progress and they are also the solution to it.**

For example, if you ask Congolese with victim mentality why they are living in much poverty and insecurity, they will say that it is because of many civil wars and militias movements that took place in their country – and they have nothing to do to improve their daily – the responsibility of what happened to them is for the political leaders and they are the ones to do every possible thing to improve the lives of the citizens.

- ✓ **People with VM strongly believe to be innocent and strongly blame other people and the circumstances they went through or their present unpleasant situations.**

For example, if they are Hutu of Rwanda in refuge– they will regret and say that their flight from Rwanda was caused by the Tutsi extremists who wanted to kill them during the genocide! And the Tutsi who have lost some of their relatives will say that they are victims of the genocide due to the Hutu extremists initiated and organized the genocide.

- ✓ **They are passive and enjoy being like that – Never or rarely come back to positive and normal attitude after shock or loss.**

In Uganda for example, as it was showed in one of the preceding chapters, millions of people who were victims of the civil war led by Joseph Kony with the LRA rebel movement – some might have developed the 'victim mentality' are still suffering from it today and some might have a quick recovery and understood that losses may happen but are not the end of everything! So, the people who might not have cope with the period of atrocious acts of Joseph Kony and go back to the normal mental attitudes of their brains constitute potential threats to durable peace and prosperity of Uganda and of the whole African Great Lakes Region. The people of the region, particularly the political leaders, should not ignore that.

✓ **Have hatred for people or things they think or accuse made them victims.**

This is a very serious dangerous outcome of the long-lasting conflicts of the AGLR; many victims have kept seeds of hatred in their hearts and minds that are likely to dwell in them for eternity! I met with a Rwandan woman of about 55 years old in Malawi in a refugee concentration camp in 2013; that woman was of Hutu Ethnic group and had suffered for a long period with victim mentality syndrome that was explained by the hatred she had about the Tutsi.

During my conversation with her, I asked her some questions concerning her experience about the 1994 Rwandan Genocide. She told me that the genocide had created in her a serious problem which did not allow her to stay in peace when meeting with people who look like Tutsi. Every black person with 'long noise similar to Tutsi' was her enemy when meeting with such people her hatred was activated as said by the woman! She told me that the solution to that problem was the prayer and fasting of three days that she organized pleading with God to curse her from that disease which was little by little going locking her in a room for unwilling to cooperate or work with people of long noise.

That is why hating people you think are responsible for your failure or trouble is unhealthy to you. It will never help you to progress towards self-realization which also important for durable peace and prosperity. We need to work with others to live well; even the people we think are the authors of our misery.

✓ **People with VM think that others are better off than them – are happier or luckier than them – (the 'why only them' question seems to be permanent in their minds).**

Most of time, when I talk to some people of the neighboring countries of DRC about prosperity, most of them always mention that their countries are not so rich to help their citizens to prosper. They say that the poverty of their countries cannot allow them to live better lives and that the Congolese of the DRC are better off than them. Some put, 'I wish I were a Congolese; there are too much gold and silver there!' Others say, 'I only I can go to DRC, my life can change for better because the land is extremely large and so favorable for agriculture.'

In Tanzania, someone said to me, "You Congolese, why do you live your country and come to Tanzania while it is naturally rich than ours… You would better stay there and fight hard to protect the riches you have there. If only I was born in the DRC, my life would be more improved than here!" His statement was showing that most of them are victims 'by nationality' (by being born in naturally poor regions).

And in Malawi, a certain Burundian told me, "when the insecurity and militias activities are over in the DRC, I can prefer to be resettled in that country because there much to do there than in our country and the people there did not suffer as we did in Burundi" These are some of the statements we hear people of different African nations say about DRC. They just assume that although all the countries of the Central Region of Africa are victims of colonization, Congolese are happier and luckier than any other people of the region. They seem to ignore that no matter what quantity of natural resources a country may have if the minds of its leaders and some of its citizens have a certain abnormality, things cannot work for the benefit of the population.

The minds of the majority of people especially the leaders should be in totally in good health to produce seeds and fruits of durable peace and prosperity for all regardless the amounts of its natural riches; that is important to know because riches does not create durable peace and prosperity for all, but the mindsets of the people play crucial role to achieve that for a nation.

✓ **They blame other people and often find ways to justify their state, and they can also lie to have good explanations to others.**

This characteristic of slave mentality addresses the mentality of many people especially some managers and leaders in the AGLR. For example, if we study carefully what many political leaders of the AGLR say and do, we can conclude that they are not good leaders and need to go to intercessory prayers or psychological counseling to be cured of the 'slave mentality syndrome'. Unfortunately, it seems that many can never acknowledge they suffer from that illness. For important national or regional projects that they failed to achieve because of their own mentality, they always find ways to justify themselves and the most famous ones are blame and lies. They are victims of their mindsets, and they are not willing to agree with that reality.

Kets de Vries (2012, p.4) puts "The blame game is part of victims' repertoire. Although their own actions are responsible for whatever situation they find themselves in, they are very talented at finding excuses why things don't work out. A common means of getting their way is to lay guilt trips on others through various kinds of emotional blackmail (Simon, 1996). They will sulk, pout, withdraw, bungle, make excuses, and lie. Their talent at sending mixed messages catches others off guard. With these people we can never be entirely sure what was said or what is expected."

- ✓ **They have a constant need for help but most of the time fail to use adequately what is offered to them in terms.**

Kets de Vries (2012) explains well that symptom in the following passage, "It is hard to ignore constant cries for help. In most instances, however, the help given is of short duration. Like moths in a flame, helpers quickly get burned; nothing seems to work to alleviate the victims' miserable situation; there is no movement for the better. Any efforts rescuers make are ignored, belittled, or met with hostility. No wonder that the rescuers become increasingly frustrated – and walk away (Worschel, 1984; Kets de Vries, 2010).

Of course, the essential question is why these 'victims' are asking for help in the first place. Do they really want to be helped? Given the endless holes they keep on digging for themselves, they may just be looking for attention. And even negative attention is better than no attention at all. We notice how the victim style becomes a relational mode – a life-affirming activity: I am miserable therefore I am. This is a common scenario for people prone to the victim syndrome." (p. 6).

- **These following questions may help find out if a person victim mentality.**

   ✓ Do you think that everyone else in the AGLR has a better life than you have?

   ✓ Do you always complain about the problems or difficulties you went through or you are undergoing now?

✓ Do you often blame others for your problems and troubles rather than thinking about practical solutions for solving them?

✓ Do you most of time find ways of justifying your failures and troubles instead of exposing them to yourself so that you figure out ways to a successful live?

✓ Do you always need help or assistance and after getting it you fail to adequately use it for your own well-being and that of others because somebody did wrong to you in the past?

✓ Do you have negative opinions about yourself due to your present miserable situation?

✓ Do you frequently focus on bad or sad events that happened in your life?

✓ Do you seem to feel very well or happy when people declare you are innocent?

✓   Do you often use lies to get the approval of other people about what happened or what is happening to you now so you don't need to do anything to change it?

These are just some of the questions we can think about when addressing the victim mentality. In the AGLR, lives need to be improved but not without change of victim mentality in people's daily thoughts, talks, and actions.

7.2.3. African Colonization Mentality (ACM)

"Never be bullied into silence. Never allow yourself to be made a victim. Accept no one's definition of your life, define yourself." (Harvey Fierstein)

What is 'African Colonization Mentality' (ACM)? How do some Africans appear to behave like Colonialists towards their fellows Africans?

It can be surprising for many people to learn that many regions of Africa are still under colonization run by the Africans themselves. It concerns mainly some groups of

African leaders who without nationalism and sense of humanism decide to take in hostage the citizens of their circumscriptions or regions in order to maintain exaggerated social, religious, economic, and political supremacy over them. These people claim in public to be nationalists with good projects to support the people but they do just the contrary of what they said as that was the case of Leopold II in the Congo (DRC).

> "But while slavery is not new, neither are efforts to stop it. An anti-slavery campaign at the end of the 19th century broke Leopold's grip on Congo. Today, human rights workers in Congo's war-afflicted east, supported by activists in North America and Europe, work to end the widespread abuses of rape, slavery, and wanton killing. Nonetheless, the dynamics of slavery and how the slavery of eastern Congo fits into contemporary legal definitions of slavery are not well understood. There is no doubt, however, that this is slavery—the control of people using violence and its threat to extract work or sexual exploitation, a radical diminution of free will, intentional coercion to make the victims believe they cannot walk away, and no pay beyond subsistence, if that. Armed groups are the principal perpetrators, but they are not alone. Civilian middle managers, moneylenders, brothel owners, and even parents in some cases, are

also responsible for these modern forms of slavery." (Free the Slave & Open Square Foundation, 2011, p. 5).

Those African Colonialists or the African people with 'Africans Colonization Mentality' (ACM) are ready to perform any atrocious acts to achieve their egoistic aims while at the same time serving the as useful agents that maintain their fellow Africans under the yoke of 'Afro-colonialism'. People with such mentality in Africa constitute a permanent threat to durable peace and prosperity for all. They have certain characteristics that are often hidden from the public eyes but can easily be noticed when scrutinized carefully. People with ACM have the mindsets with a number of fake ideas among them the following can be mentioned.

✓ They wrongly feel like they are very superior to others.

- ✓ They have no too much hope all the time and are ready to reach it by any possible mean (even by using violence and dishonest ways).

- ✓ They are in bondage by the 'European Colonial ideologies' that they continue to use (they are slaves of colonial destructive colonial ideas).

- ✓ They put people in bandage with the same colonial ideas by imposing poverty and ignorance to the general population to eternally have dominance over them.

- ✓ They totally depend on Western donors and on what they get dishonesty (no personal and constructive imitative for durable peace and prosperity for all).

- ✓ They don't believe in the power of respecting human rights and the laws of their respective nations.

- ✓ They deprive people of their freedom and are fearful of any new idea and opposition parties.

- ✓ They have much doubt and suspicion of people who try to initiative some socioeconomic activities of national or regional interests for all.

- ✓ They fight with much force for power and money, and hate any foreign and national investors who are not ready to give them corruption.

- ✓ They dislike any human right activist and are ready to harm or kill them in some circumstances.

- ✓ They strongly have any person who is not ready to 'worship' them for they think of themselves as gods or mystically descendants of gods.

These are some of the ideas the 'Black Africans Colonialists' have about themselves. That is why the consequences of their acts are very destroying and will always block any possible process towards durable peace and prosperity for all if there is no change at all.

Consequences of Africans Colonization Mentality (ACM)

✓ **Serious Violation of Human Rights and the Laws of the Country**

Like Leopold II and other White Colonialists, the African Masters with the mentality of colonization do not consider Africans as people who have rights that should be respected. They don't see them as human beings with equal dignity and responsibility. These black masters are very perilous; they have grave lack of respect for people who are not of their class. They can easily kill, rape, take people in hostage, plunder, manipulate others, etc.

The laws of the countries they live in do not mean anything to them. They are very rude and think to be above the laws. Their exaggerated pride and riches accumulated dishonestly make them think that they are safe and unchangeable. They say for example to others "I can kill you and pay for that! You are nothing on my eyes!" The category of black African Maters of colonization in the AGLR include but limited to the leaders of militias involved in the illegal exploitation of minerals in the DRC, the leaders of rebel movements who forcibly use anyone to achieve their goals (even children), the political leaders who use people like objects (things) to satisfy their egoistic thirst of power and riches, the people who are always ready to kill their relatives or neighbors for money or power, the government members who willingly don't respect or make respect the laws of the country and the Universal Declaration of Human Rights (UDHR), the presidents who have the penchant to eternalize themselves on power while their mandates are over, the religious leaders who are leading churches without any initiatives that can help their adepts to prosperity, etc.

These people fear to move freely in their countries; they don't feel like they are so safe because of the attitudes and acts that violate the rights of others. For instance, in some countries like DRC, you can see a political or military authority move with a huge number of bodyguards on their own territory as if they are going to a battle somewhere! That is because they have established themselves as Masters over the citizens who have become their slaves and they have been violating their rights for so long that they feel like everybody is their enemy.

Most of these people with 'black African colonization mentality' are trained out of the African continent where they developed the feeling that they had become superior to other Africans because of their training and experience in more developed countries! That may be considered as one of the facts that push them to disrespect the rights of others, and think higher of themselves.

Gabriel (2014, p.80) mentions something similar to what I have called ACM in the minds of some African leaders in the following passage.

> "In other words the prototypes, modalities and operations of the development needed for Africa is located in the African continent; in its culture, tradition, religion, philosophy, language, environment and so forth. On the contrary, however, the African journey to the development it envisages today began from the internal arrangement and purpose of the continent; informed by the schemes of external predators and its destination is located somewhere beyond its shores whence its driving force and leading light came. The African agents of this development if they are humans were isolated from their local communities, trained elsewhere to gaze upon their community with air of superiority and disgust. Within their training they learned to reject their language, culture, religion and even their names; they get initiated into the process by being emptied of who they were to take on a new personality. Their

training informs them that they are becoming more like their trainers; and because they have also been goaded to accede to the superiority of their trainers, this in turn informs their superiority-complex and that their local environment is base and of no good; this in its own turn also informs their acquired disgust for it. While they were away, their trainers continued to vandalize and impoverish their homeland. … The war of Europe against Africa is a war of mentality and in it the African spirit was the target and has been wounded in various fronts." (p. 80).

✓ Creating and Reviving Conflict and Divisions among People.

As one of the best strategies of the colonialists during the colonial era of Africa, 'dividing people' in order to have more power over them is the frequent act of the African Masters of ACM today. These people whose aims are nothing but to have dominion over human beings and to possess all good things for themselves and then give some to the agents who worship them, hate all persons, movements, clubs, groups, political parties, civil societies, congregations, etc. who enlighten the minds of the generation population by providing them useful information or advice that can make them become united durable peace and prosperity for all. They make sure true information that can help find against ignorance is hidden to the average citizens so that they can remain in the darkness.

Because they know that if the majority of the people have access to the correct information and become united to fight for their rights, they can claim for their mental independence; that is what the colonialists are not willing to give them. And when people are not united, their power to fight together diminishes; they remain powerless and continue to eternally depend on their fellow black Africans who do not want them to live in prosperity.

✓ **Plundering the riches in Africa and their transfer in West for Safe-keeping**

This is another eloquent characteristic of African masters of colonization in Africa today. These people with African colonization mind seem to have no pity of their own nations. They still huge amounts of money from governments, public institutions, churches, missionaries, congregations, ministries, etc. to enrich themselves in detriment to the projects that are meant to help many people and sometimes the whole nation. The worst reality about that is the fact that the African leaders with such mentality transfer large sums of money to Western countries for 'safe keeping' even the funds that are given by western donors to support the lives of millions of Africans who are living in serious poverty.

In the AGLR, many political leaders invest much money in foreign countries especially in Western ones; much of what is sent there is illegally or dishonestly gained in detriment to the general population that they lead! How can African people live in durable peace and prosperity with leaders who have the mentality of plundering the riches of their respective countries and then keep them in the foreign countries? Isn't crazy to still the money donated by Westerners in order to help the poor African governments and sent it back in a private account for 'safe keeping'?

Can African leaders with such mentality consider themselves to be truly Africans or they are more dangerous to African continent than the Leopold II and his agents? People involved in such activities should stop so that durable peace and prosperity for all may be effective.

It will be a shame and endless misery for African if, after having been colonized by non-Africans, some of Africans are systematically organizing colonial activities in Africa which are more destructive than before the independence era of the continent.

✓ **Forced labor**

The 'black African colonialists' also force others to work without or with very little earnings. They know that any person who works deserves a salary, but they never give salaries to people. They only offer to their workers a very little gain that can help them survive while working hard. Most of what is given to the colonized workers are packets of inappropriate and insufficient food items or very few money that buy it.

That is why in many regions of Africa, especially in the AGLR, we find many people who have been working for others for many years but they have a poor physical health due to the food shortage or malnutrition! These enslaved worked who are forced to work by the worse life circumstances imposed to them by the black African bosses with colonizing mentality. No matter what type or level of education and experience a person has, as long as they are under 'the forced labor system in the AGLR', their suffering increase day after day because of they cannot live adequate lives by the fruits of their work.

That is another form of robbery that is used by some politicians in power, some religious leaders, some leaders involved in commerce, some heads of departments, and almost all the rebel movements' leaders (militia leaders). These groups of people constitute a terrible menace to any possible process of durable peace and prosperity for all in the African Great Lakes Region. What they are doing in forcing people to work for them, directly using guns or any other threat or indirectly by putting them into difficult constitutions of life, is sometimes unnoticed by the general populations or the organizations advocating for the respect of human rights.

The White European Colonialists had the same mentality that is why the AGLR, although its rich natural resources and capable population, have been suffering from serious socioeconomic crisis since colonial period up to nowadays.

- ✓ **Apparently Good Cooperation with Religious Leaders or Missionaries**

Some religious leaders and missionaries are still accepting to serve the 'Africans colonialists' agendas of putting heavy loads on the population in order to serve their egoistic interests. By the means of brides or other forms of influencing people, some religious African leaders are serving as catalysts to the destructive goals of the unconscious Africans who are decided to continue colonization on their own native lands.

The missionaries of the time of Leopold II did that compulsory, but some some religious leaders in Africa today seem to be doing that willingly to have riches or to gain the support or approvals from authorities and bosses of the countries in which they are working. This is so alarming because some of what is happening today seem to be more dangerous and destructive than what happened in the past. And what is very tricky and make it unnoticed by the national or international opinion is that mostly those nonconstructive acts take place in secret!

For example, to make sure their unjust and colonial supremacy is maintained over their adepts, some religious leaders have been teaching that in the life of human beings some possessions are purely secular and some others are spiritual. And the spiritual is more important, and is not often concerned with the search of materials (possessions), honor, and personal respect. The spiritual are so important, and people should love what is spiritual and unseen more than what is seen. Why? 'If you love what is seen and work hard to gain materials for yourself, you will not go to heaven when you die; rich people don't go to heaven when they die!'

More often than not, the religious leaders behind the scenes in the 'Black Africans' colonization of Africans' work hard to maintain the status quo. They preach to their followers to accept the present situation rather than helping them to find a way towards positive change. For example, believers are asked to offer to God or gods (to through their religious leaders), the most valuable things they have as a mean of purchasing or securing their personal houses in heaven (paradise). That kind of teaching maintains many religious followers in a situation of durable socioeconomic insecurity and poverty instead of helping them to set on the paths of durable peace and prosperity. With that situation the religious followers who are also citizens will be in a situation of permanent ignorance and poverty that will never allow them to access to the truth to set them free from the yoke of the black African colonialist leaders.

However, some Africans have been able to see the peace and prosperity killing religious principles that have been taught Africans since the colonial era up to nowadays but unable to refute it. "It is difficult, confusing, and often painful for the African to learn that Christians seem to regard some things as spiritual and some others as 'secular,' separated fairly sharply from the spiritual. To African traditional thought and action such a division does not make sense. It is a negation of the facts of life as he and his fathers have observed and lived it from generations. Life to him is a unity guided and almost always controlled by the spirit." (Ross, 2013, p.202).

Keim (2013, p.9) writes "Although the United States never ruled colonies in Africa, Americans did enslave Africans and maintain both a slavery system and segregation. Moreover, we profited from our businesses in Africa, sent missionaries to change African culture, and did not protest the colonization undertaken by Europeans. This exploitation of Africa, whether direct or indirect, required thinking about Africans as inferiors."

7.2.4. Black African Racism Mentality (BARM) – Black Africans against Africans

"Being black is not a matter of pigmentation – being black is a reflection of a mental attitude."
(Stephen Bantu Biko)

What is 'Black African Racism Mentality' (BARM)?

In this book, what is called 'Black African Racism Mentality' is the African mindsets of considering people of different physical shapes, cultures, native languages, ethnicity, geographical dwelling place, etc. as naturally inferior or unequal in terms of rights and opportunities. The BARM is very treacherous because it creates barriers to black African people's social interactions among themselves. And when people cannot interact well, their progress towards durable peace and prosperity will suffer many negative facts like negative stereotypes, negative attitudes, negative talks, etc.

The AGLR is peopled mainly by black people; the issue of different races in the region may seem to be neglected there because of the fact that all tribes and ethnic groups are black. But the reality in day to day people's interactions is contrary to what many may think about the AGLR. It seems that many people in the AGLR conceive 'racism' based on a number of physical traits (life the shape of the noise), ethnicity, tribes, social status and regional belonging (geographical place where a person lives – regionalism), type of mother language people speak, etc. and not just the color of the skin or type of hair as many may believe.

Defining race, Wolf (nd, p.1) puts "Race is a socially constructed artifact that categorizes people based on visual differences which are imputed to indicate invisible differences. These categorizations are amorphous and fluid over time which reflects their social rather than physical basis." From this definition, we can understand it is the mentality of people that push them to judge others by what they see on their physical appearances. About racism, Dr. Rowan Wolf writes that it can be defined 'simply as any policy, belief, attitude, action or inaction, which subordinates individuals or groups based on their race (Wolf, nd, p. 2).

What people think and believe about others is not always the truth; racism is insanity because of its power to set people apart. Racism will never a nation in poverty and misery to set its paths towards peace and prosperity because of the segregation it imposes on people. Racism between back Africans themselves has resulted in very dangerous and atrocious acts than the racism between the White colonialists and the Black Africans during the colonial era. And this reality has been made possible by the contribution of some religious congregation with their free will contrary to the African missionaries that were forced to do the same by Leopold II!

For example, during the Rwanda Genocide in 1994, some religious leaders have used the Bible to justify and propagate the massive killing initiative among the populations. They showed people that the Tutsi ethnic group was a race cursed by God; that they were snakes. They used biblical passages to achieve their genocidal acts. To justify the massive killings of Tutsi in Rwanda, Christian Hutu preachers invoked what King Saul did with direct reference to the story of the Bible (Jenkins, 2011). "What seems to Africans as color discrimination exists in almost all parts of Africa, brought chiefly by the Christian West." (Ross, 2013, p.202). Should Black Africans discriminate against Black Africans only because somebody showed them that they are different and unequal? Should they kill each other because for that? Should they accept such ugly lies by people with BARM?

We really need a positive change of mind on personal consideration of people who have different morphology than us, of people who speak a different native language from ours, of people who have different cultural beliefs from ours, of people with different ways of doing things in life. Can you imagine a group of ethnic leaders who write down a set of racist commandments to be used against another ethnic group? During the genocidal conflict in Rwanda, there have been redaction and propagation of commandments called the 'Hutu Ten Commandments' resumed in the following.

- Every Hutu male should know that Tutsi women, wherever they may be, are working in the pay of their Tutsi ethnic group. Consequently, shall be deemed a traitor:

  ✗ Any Hutu male who marries a Tutsi woman;

  ✗ Any Hutu male who keeps a Tutsi concubine;

  ✗ Any Hut male who makes a Tutsi woman his secretary or protégée.

- Every Hutu male must know that our Hutu daughters are more dignified and conscientious in their role of women, wife or mother. Are they not pretty, good secretaries and more honest!

- Hutu women, be vigilant and bring your husbands, brothers and sons back to their senses.

- Every Hutu male must know that all Tutsi are dishonest in their business dealings. They are only seeking their ethnic supremacy. "Time will tell." Shall be considered a traitor, any Hutu male:

  ✗ who enters into a business partnership with Tutsi;

  ✗ who invests his money or State money in a Tutsi company;

  ✗ who lends to, or borrows from, a Tutsi;

- ✘ who grants business favors to Tutsi (granting of important licenses, bank loans, building plots, public tenders…) is a traitor.
- Strategic position in the political, administrative, economic, military and security domain should, to a large extent, be entrusted to Hutu.
- In the education sector (pupils, students, teachers) must be in the majority Hutu.
- The Rwandan Armed Forces should be exclusively Hutu. That is the lesson we learned from the October 1990 war. No soldier must marry a Tutsi woman.
- Hutu must cease having pity for the Tutsi.
- The Hutu male, wherever he may be, must be united, in solidarity and be concerned about the fate of their Hutu brothers;
  - ✘ The Hutu at home and abroad must constantly seek friends and allies for the Hutu Cause, beginning with our Bantu brothers;
  - ✘ They must constantly counteract Tutsi propaganda;
  - ✘ The Hutu must be firm and vigilant towards their common Tutsi enemy.

- The 1959 social revolution, the 1961 referendum and the Hutu ideology must be taught to Hutu at all levels. Every Hutu must propagate the present ideology widely. Any Hutu who persecutes his Hutu brother for having read, disseminated and taught this ideology shall be deemed a traitor.

The editor of the journal Kangura, Hassan Ngeze, was said to be the author of the 'The Hutu Ten Commandments', and in 2003 was convicted by the International Criminal Tribal for Rwanda (ICTR) of genocide and crimes against humanity (Southgate, 2011).

The Hutu ten commandments aimed nothing but to destroy Rwanda and the whole African Great Lakes Region. The authors and propagandists of these commandments seemed to be ignoring that their mentality was against their own prosperity and the peace of the whole AGLR by the fact that the Tutsi are not the citizens of Rwanda only; they also live in Burundi, Uganda, and DR Congo. People sometimes dig a hole for themselves to fall in the future without knowing it at all. That is not different from the mentality of a person who is sawing the legs of a chair on which they are seated. We depend on each other to live in durable peace and prosperity regardless our differences.

Other shocking 'Black Africans racial' events took place in the DR Congo between the Lendu and Hema of Ituri – ethnic groups in the Province of Haut Congo – in militia movements. During the period of 1998 – 2003, militia groups called Union of Congolese Patriots (UPC) led by Thomas Lubanga and the Patriotic Forces for the Liberation of Congo (FPLC) were responsible for many atrocities in the war they organized in Ituri. In the Ituri region where ethnic conflicts prevailed since long ago, the UPC rebel movement claimed to represent the Hema. From 2002 to 2003, it was reported by the human rights activists that the FPLC had killed about 800 Lendu civilians with the order given by Thomas Lubanga.

There were also rapes of women, torture of innocent people, and kidnapping of children forced to serve as child-solders. This is how the Black African Racists treat people of different ethnic groups and tribes with so much hate. They don't treat them as human beings possessing rights that should be strictly respected. There is always a historical explanation to almost all the tribal or ethnic conflicts exploited by Black African Racists to justify their atrocious acts against the other tribe or ethnic group. What is sad at this point is that most of the time people rely on false or irrational and illogical historic facts and information to create and nurture peace-killing tribal and ethnic conflicts.

That is one of the strategies used by people with black African racism mentality; if you cannot change a positive impact to their lives by teaching or advising them, you should be careful with them because they are so dangerous by their capacity to plant the seeds of tribal or ethnic conflicts in the minds of others. Thomas Lubanga, who was accused of crime against humanity and of reviving the dormant conflict between Hema and Lendu and by violating the rights of many citizens in Ituri, was finally arrested by the Congolese authorities in March 2005. And later on, Lubanga was transferred to International Criminal Court.

According to the history of DRC, it is known that the roots of the conflict between the Hema and Lendu in Ituri have reasons grounded on the access on land, economic resources, and political positions. As it was the case of

Tutsi in Rwanda and Burundi, the Belgian colonialists favored the Hema in detriment to the Lendu in Ituru. The Hema become powerful economically than the Lendu who claim that the lands belong to them historically as is also the case of the Hutu in Rwanda and Burundi. About that, Vlassenroot and Raeymaekers (2003, p. 3 – 4) writes,

> "The political economy of social fragmentation in Ituri is the outcome of a long historic process, in which internal and external elements became intertwined. As elsewhere in eastern Congo, the Belgian colonial administration relied on one local ethnic community (the Hema) for its administration based on the principle of indirect rule, to the disadvantage of the other local ethnic communities. As a consequence, the Hema found themselves in a favored position after independence: not only did they acquire easy access to the plantations left by the Belgian settlers, but also to political positions. Mobutu's principle of stratification – converting political loyalty into economic assets – required the regular recycling of the political elite, under his proverbial divide-and-rule strategy, but also enabled the Hema to consolidate their local economic and political domination. At several occasions other ethnic communities (mainly the Lendu) resisted against this Hema-domination, claiming the original historical land ownership.

> Until the second half of the nineties, however, these conflicts never escalated into full-scale violence. It was only after the Kabila-led AFDL-rebellion (1996-1997), and the subsequent internal political void, that local elites tried to strengthen their power-position. Their search for allies, in concurrence with the divide-and-rule tactics of Ugandan army commanders, has led to the first eruption of violence in 1999." (p. 3 – 4).

The conflict was there but almost dead. As it was the case of Rwanda where the FPR had the support of Uganda during the year 1994, so it was with the UPC in 1998; both wars resulted in racial massive killings although the reality of Rwanda is almost different from that of Ituri. The populations of the African Great Lakes Region need to open the eyes to clearly see who their exact enemies are; the people who are against the durable peace and prosperity for all need to be identified because the citizens who are always victims and sometimes supporters of destroyers need to stop and change their mentality.

Characteristics of people with 'Black African Racism Mentality' (BARM)

In the African Great Lakes Region (AGLR), people with 'Black African Racism Mentality' have some of the following traits.

- They consider themselves as true Africans (the veritable Africans) whose ancestors might have been descendants of people with similar personal and physical traits with the ancestors of Westerners of today or had noble natural character different from that of the ancestors of the other Africans of different tribes or ethnic groups.

- They hate people of different tribes, ethnic groups, regions; they think of their cultures as being the best.

- They have exaggerated attachment and love for the provinces or region where they were born and disgust for people of other regions.

- They have a tendency to impose their mother languages or cultures to other people of ethnic groups or tribes.

- They like to associate only with people of their ethnic groups, tribes, regions, or villages.

- Almost the majority of the jobs in their governments, companies, congregations, etc. are given to people of their tribes, ethnic groups, regions, or villages.

- They only marry people of their ethnic groups or tribes and they encourage other to do that.

- They lead associations, political parties, governments, etc. on the basis of their racist discriminative principles.

- They don't regret at all if people of different ethnic groups, tribes, regions die regardless the social ties they had with them.

- They only vote for the people of their own ethnic groups, tribes, region, or village even if they don't qualify to be elected (even if they are not competent).

- They also organize propaganda based on the hate and negative criticism for other tribes and ethnic groups.

- They think that other tribes or ethnic groups are worthless and all their members belong to the lower class regardless their social standing.

- They also think that violating the rights of people of different tribes or ethnic groups or killing them is not a sin at all.

- Their minds are favorable for genocidal teachings or propaganda making them ready to initiate or take part in genocides.

Elements of "Black African Racism Mentality"

In the AGLR, the 'Black African Racism Mentality' in the societies by the ethnic discrimination, hate or disdain for people of different tribes (tribalism), favor towards the people of one's village or family only (Nepotism), and collaboration or cooperation based on regions (regionalism).

• Ethnic discrimination

The discrimination based on ethnic group belonging prevails in the African Great Lakes Region of Africa. This region in Africa has too many 'Black African Racists' who fight against the people of their own nations who do not belong to their ethnic groups. Their fight is sometimes cold and invisible to the masses – the one that cannot be openly seen without a careful scrutiny – and result in what can be called 'cold violence'; and sometimes it produces easily visible and direct consequences on people of different ethnic groups.

What had been happening in Rwanda, Burundi, and DRC, from 1990 up to 2007, was not just the result of serious hate and discrimination based on ethnic belonging. The world called them 'genocides'; and the looser were and are still the peoples of the AGLR. It is time to stop such mindset. Millions of people died even the innocent babies were slaughtered as it is showed in the following drawing.

Also, the stories that we hear from some Rwandan refugees who had worked in Rwanda during the post-genocide period convey some information that may be considered as an illustration to the 'cold violence' based on ethnic discrimination there. During the year 2014, I met with a certain guy who fled from Rwanda after working there for the period following the 1994 genocide. This man belonged to the Hutu Ethnic group and for security reason he did not want his name to be mentioned in any publication. He said to me "I was very shocked when they told me at the airport that I was not supposed to go to the professional training abroad only because I am a 'Hutu'. I was considered as 'half-human being' because of the shape of my nose, because of my race. Because of what happened to me I don't prefer to work with the Tutsi anymore. There is too much ethnic discrimination in Rwanda which is not really noticed by some national and international observers."

While some people may tell lies to deteriorate the reputation of others but the truth with the AGLR is that some leaders discriminate based on ethnic belonging. And that will never help the region to fully achieve durable peace and prosperity. There is a need for positive change for those who are still discrimination others because of some differences of physical traits, culture, or language.

For example, ethnic belonging should not be among the criteria for recruitment in the government organizations, private companies, and religious organizations. Such mentality makes fragile the community initiatives for durable peace and prosperity for all. It is one of the poisonous attitudes that make peace impossible in communities of the AGLR although numerous programs and activities initiated and funded to achieve it for all.

- **Hate or Discrimination based on Region ("Regionalism")**

During the period post-genocidal in Rwanda, apart from ethnic discrimination, there was also a discrimination based on regional belonging. For example, a Hutu old woman who lived in the political environment of late President of Rwanda Habyarimana, said to that the Hutu of the Southern Rwanda were not cooperating well with the Hutu of the North. And what she said about that is the fact that even in the countries where those people go to seek refugee they still discriminate based on regional belonging or province of origin.

The Hutu people of the north of Rwanda were mostly loyal to Habyarimana. He was from their region, and those of the south were supporters of Kahibanda's ideology. And the discrimination among some of these people is still actual today even in foreign countries. This is also the case of Burundi. In September 2015 in Malawi, a certain refugee woman from Burundi told me this "in Burundi, I originate in the province of Chibitoke – before I led the country, we were difficultly working or cooperating with the people of other provinces. For example, the people of Rumonge do not speak Kirundi as we do; there are some differences of accents and that make most people in our province think that we are not the same people. So, we discriminate each other; even here in Malawi that is happening among some Burundians."

This is a socially institutionalized disease that needs to be eradicated among the people of the AGLR so that any program or project of peace and prosperity for all may run healthy and benefit the populations. But do the people with that mentality know it is socially detrimental to consider others unequal only because they belong to different regions, provinces? Or they find it okay and are ready to continue teaching it to their progenitors?

Also, in the DR Congo, among the people who like in Kinshasa – capital city of the country – there are some who treat the people from other regions or provinces of the country with disdain. They call them 'Bato ya Interieur' (people of the bushes). They also consider themselves to be more civilized than the people of other provinces. They mock at the people of the Eastern provinces of the country.

- **Tribalism**

Tribalism is another form of manifestation of 'Black African Racism Mentality'. In the context of the AGLR, tribalism can be defined as the mentality of considering one's tribe as the best of all tribes; therefore the tribal members should work for the egoistic benefits of their own tribe in detriment of other existing tribes in the country, province, town, territory, village.

Is it because of the traditional belief that the members of a tribe share a common ancestry? Or it their racism mentality that pushes them to be more focused and sometimes only on their tribes by ignoring others? It is and will remain a pity for the AGLR if people will not accept to abandon most of their harmful traditional ways of living.

We are now living in the modern time where some traditional beliefs and practices need to be put aside in order to cope with this aching and fast developing world. Since the world had stopped to be a geographic, anthropological, and geologic mystery and has become a village with the advancement of globalization, people who need durable peace and prosperity especially those of AGLR should consider the world's population as one tribe.

That is one large tribe in one large village with a very rich diversity in terms of languages, skin colors, cultures, etc. I am an African writing about this negative African mentality but some other non-Africans know that some Africans live in tribes. For example, the popular American view about Africa is clearly seen in the following quote.

> "And although most Americans do not possess many facts about Africa, we do know certain general truths about the continent. We know, for example, that Africans live in tribes. And we know that Africa is a place of famine, disease, poverty, coups, and large wild animals." (Keim, 2013, p.7).

For those who will not accept to break the barriers caused by tribal discrimination in AGLR, there will always times of troubles due to their unimportant attachment to their personal tribes or tribal propaganda aiming to create division among the people. Even thinking of having the same traditional ancestor should not be the cause of tribal discrimination among the people because that one was a human being who had siblings and parents to be believed authors of some other tribes.

As it was shown in the introduction of this book, Christianity has very higher percentage of adepts in the AGLR than any other religion. If all the Christians in the region really believe what their sacred book (Bible) says about the origin of human beings and propagate it to other people there could be a certain change in some people mentality about tribalism. The Bible puts "Then God said, 'And now we will make human beings; they will be like us and resemble us. They will have power over the fish, the birds, and all animals, domestic and wild, large and small.' So God created human beings, making them to be like himself. He created them male and female," (Genesis 1:26 – 27). "Then the Lord God took some soil from the ground and formed a man out of it; he breathed life-giving breath into his nostrils and the man began to live." (Genesis 2:7).

And another biblical passage puts "From one human being he created all races on earth and made them live throughout the whole earth. He himself fixed beforehand the exact times and the limits of the places where they would live. He did this so that they would look for him, and perhaps find him as they felt about for him. Yet God is actually not far from anyone of us;" (Acts 17:26 – 27). Do all the Christians in the AGLR understand well these biblical passages? Are some of them involved in tribal discrimination with this biblical knowledge? They need to stop as it is put clear their by the Bible.

Even Muslims share the same beliefs about creation and they represent the second high percentage of people in the AGLR after the Christians. If the teachings of Christianity and Islam about the origin of human beings are hard to believe for some in the region, researches and discoveries of scientists are eloquent to ban 'Black African Racism Mentality'.

For those who will not believe the story of the Bible about Adam and Eve may think about why the scientists are discovering facts that seem to be similar to what the Bible teaches concerning the issue of descending from a common ancestry. "When scientists announced their 'discovery' of Eve last year, they rekindled perhaps the oldest human debate: where did we come from? They also, in some sense, confirmed a belief that existed long before the Bible. Versions of the Adam-and-Eve story date back at least 5,000 years and have been told in cultures from the Mediterranean to the South Pacific to the Americas." (Tiernney, & Wright, & Springen, 2013, p. 65).

We are not trying to ask the reader of this book to be adept of any religious teaching by following what they say about the origin of human being; the point here is to have a clear understanding of the equality of humans regardless their tribes and races based on the fact that they might have been descending from a common ancestry. That is why racial, ethnic, or tribal discrimination is insanity. Fade (2013, p.47) inscribes "The earliest known evidence anywhere in the world for the existence of man and the emergence of human society comes from the East and

North-East Africa, from a serious of discoveries that stem from Dr. Louis Leakey's pioneer excavations at Olduvai Gorge in northern Tanzania. Later finds, by the Lake Turkana in Kenya and the river Omo in Ethiopia, for example, have taken the story of human evolution in Africa even further into the past."

And the following quote also informs that apart from what was discovered in Africa about first parents of human race some laboratories in the USA have something to say.

> "This time, however, the argument involves a new breed of anthropologists who work in air-conditioned American laboratories instead of desiccated African rift valleys. Trained in molecular biology, they looked at an international assortment of genes and picked up a trail of DNA that led them to a single woman from who we are all descended. Most evidence so far indicates that Eve lived in sub-Saharan Africa, although a few researchers think her home might have been southern China." (Tierney, 1992).

If that is the region where Eve lived, we can assume that it the same for Adam because a married woman mostly lives near her husband who guarantees protection for her. So, people of the AGLR should understand that the discoveries of the scientists and the account of the Bible about the parentage of human beings are not so different at all. Instead of discriminating each other based on tribes or ethnic groups belonging, you would have been so proud of living in a region where your common ancestor is suspected to have been living.

- **Nepotism**

Nepotism is another durable peace and prosperity blocking mentality. In the AGLR, we have seen people orienting jobs and other important activities to the persons with whom they have direct or indirect relationships only because they are members of their family. On this point, we don't need to recall the long theory of leadership and management in order to make a positive and edifying argument.

Almost every person of good sense may say that it is not good to give people jobs or works which they are not able to do well. Good leaders, managers, and bosses know that their personal success depends so much on the competence of the people they employ in their organizations, in their governments. Even family companies need the right people at the right place to function successfully. It is good to mention that public institutions should be highly organized because they are very important for the prosperity of the populations of a State.

We need to acknowledge that public institutions should not be managed as if they were private properties of individuals who are working as managers or directors.

They exist by the public and for the public not for the private. People with 'Black African Racism Mentality' exhibiting the 'Nepotism symptom' will find hard to cope with this reality. After employing their unqualified relatives, they tend to consider the public organizations they lead as their private property and finally they mismanage funds and even seize all or some of the items available for public services for themselves at the end of their terms! This situation often happens in the DRC and does not allow durable peace and prosperity for all to take place.

There are always people who complain about the leadership in some public companies and even some private ones; they sometimes say "don't even waste your time writing an application letter for that organization, they only employ their relatives or people they have very strong relationship with!". Others who are working with relative top manager seem to say "when the new top manager takes the responsibility, he will come with his news employees; it is useless to work well here, let's pillage what will sustain us during the period of joblessness!" And some top managers with that mentality seem to say "We should make sure we are very safe in our work; and the best way to achieve that is to hire our relatives and faithful friends in the name of security and trust, and to make sure our bosses consider us as their relatives too!" This is very alarming for the AGLR because with such mentality durable peace and prosperity for all cannot be achieved.

7.2.5. Witchcraft or Sorcery Mentality (WSM)

"I'm not over-reacting, but I do think people have to be
a bit cautious when they say all kind of activities
associated with witchcraft are harmless."
(Peter Hollingworth)

What is Witchcraft or Sorcery in Africa?

Witchcraft and Sorcery are concepts introduced in Africa during the colonial time. Such practices existed before the colonial era, and the local concepts that matched with what was considered as Witchcraft or Sorcery by European colonialists and missionaries during the colonial period. Cimpric (2010, p.8) writes about that by showing that "the French notion of 'sorcellerie', as well as the English equivalent, 'witchcraft' and 'sorcery', were introduced in Africa by the first European explorers, colonialists and missionaries." What he mentions are just the 'words' in their two different European languages; but the practice of witchcraft or so sorcery existed in Africa before the arrival of European.

It had been and still is associated with the use of occult or mystical forces with the outcome of harming regardless the aim and reasons behind that. However, people try to make a distinction between 'Witchcraft and Sorcery' but all possible explanations about them correspond to the French concept of 'sorcellerie'. Cimpric (2010, p.9) gives certain clarification about that by putting,

> "Moreover, in English there is a further distinction between "witchcraft" and "sorcery". This distinction was introduced in the 1930s by the British anthropologist Edward E. Evans-Pritchard who was working with the Zande in Anglo-Egyptian Sudan (1937). According to Evans-Pritchard, the Zande clearly distinguished between "witchcraft" and "sorcery". For them, witchcraft referred to a substance that was inherited and innate, located in the abdomen of people called "witches"; because this substance sometimes acted independently of the witch's control, it could be considered in this case to be an unconscious act. The witch operates at night, invisible and transformed, metamorphosed or unfolded from its physical "envelop", in order to harm victims by devouring their life essence. In contrast, a sorcerer is someone who is socially recognized as such,

operating during the day and able to harm others by using plant substances and rituals associated with evil-doing. The sorcerer always acts consciously, and although his or her knowledge is not innate and may be practiced by anyone, it can nevertheless be transferred from one generation to the next."

Witchcraft or Sorcery Mentality prevails in the minds of millions of people in the AGLR. We are going to talk about it by considering two main categories of beliefs with that mentality. The first category of people with witchcraft or sorcery mentality include those who destroy peace in the community by their strong beliefs in witchcraft and sorcery and end up by accusing others of being 'witches or sorcerers'; and the second category will be about the people who believe in witchcraft or sorcery and use it to harm others and block peace and prosperity of others. Both categories of people with Witchcraft or Sorcery Mentality are so dangerous for the communities of the

African Great Lakes Region and are directly hindering durable peace and prosperity for all.

Characteristics of Witchcraft or Sorcery Mentality

People with witchcraft or sorcery mentality have the following characteristics but not limited to,

- strong beliefs in the use of witchcraft or sorcery in order to succeed in life;

- personal insecurity – much fear of doing without a charm or any other thing from the witches or sorcerers;

- spend money for consultation of witches or sorcerers;

- ready to sacrifice means, time, or human beings (killing people) to get and sustain their power by means of witchcraft or sorcery activities;

- too much jealousy – they can even kill a medical doctor while they don't have another one in their community and cannot become one – for other people and their possessions;

- suspicion – they easily suspect others and sometimes accuse, harm, or kill them – over their friends, partners, and relatives;

- instability and dislike of opposition;

- exaggerated desire to control other or to be in charge;

- sadism – they are happy when other people suffer or lose – hidden to the eyes of others;

- dissatisfaction – they are never satisfied with power, money, etc. – on a permanent basis in their daily lives.

Impact of Witchcraft or Sorcery Mentality on People of AGLR

Taking into consideration the characteristics of people with witchcraft of sorcery mentality in the AGLR, we can easily think of the results of their acts as destructive on the populations. Let's consider the two categories of people with witchcraft or sorcery mentality, those who have strong beliefs in witchcraft and sorcery and often accuse others of being 'witches or sorcerers' and those who believe in witchcraft or sorcery and use it to harm others, so let's try to examine some of the results of their mentality in communities of the AGLR. The practice of witchcraft or sorcery in African is very destructive and impossible to be taken to the court of law because of its resinous lack of proofs or evidence.

Witches and sorcerers most of time operate in an invisible ways to the human physical eyes! Because they believed to work in spiritual realms, only some people with spiritual capacity to see what is happening there can be able to see. And the courts and modern jurisdictions do not have that ability. That fact makes it very destructive and quasi-unpunished by the state officials. So, the witches and sorcerers kill people who are still needed by the societies in Africa for their development towards durable peace and prosperity for all.

Kisilu Kombo (2003, p.77) mentions some of the destructive consequences of witchcraft and sorcery in Africa by putting "The practice of witchcraft poses dangers in the society as it causes deaths of innocent people. This denies society the potential contribution that members who are so killed could have made to society.

This action creates widows, widowers and orphans as people lose their partners and offspring due to this malicious practice. In communities where such deaths occur there is increasing fear and despondency among the population when people die mysteriously. This leads to a state of confusion and suspicion. Witches are said to be jealous individuals who do not like to see others succeed in life." (Kombo, K., 2003, p. 77).

That is why any persona with the witchcraft mentality is a dangerous menace to durable peace and prosperity for all because jealousy which does not want people to live successfully is very destructive. And in Africa, the results of such mentality show how much the African societies will be facing problems hindering social development in a state of security and well-being of all. In the AGLR, the witchcraft mentality has resulted in several accusations of children of being witches robbing them their inner-peace and their rights to live harmoniously with others in the society. For example, "There are around 50,000 children being held in churches in the Democratic Republic of Congo accused of witchcraft, a BBC film team has discovered." (Osborne, 2013).

This situation often creates a peace-destructive social disorder because most of the accused children end up by being feared by other people in the communities and sometimes the 'streets become their parents'. What do they do live when they become street children if it is not robbing, harming, and in some extent killing passengers? Aren't some of these traumatized children recruited by militias to serve in their movements? If yes, what attitude will they have for their respective communities while serving their masters; can they build or destroy? Any leaders in the AGLR need to address this issue very seriously for durable peace and prosperity for all cannot walk the same way that social disease.

By arguing this way, we are not trying to show that witchcraft or sorcery exists or does not exist in the African Great Lake Region. In fact, believing in witchcraft or sorcery or not believing in it should not have any peace-troubling effects on the lives of peoples because any belief or disbelief that results in useless accusations, quarrels, fear, torture, fight, murder, and wars is negative and not healthy for a good social cohabitation. On 14th November 2014, Leo Igwe spoke about witchcraft accusation in Africa at a 'conference on witchcraft branding, spirit possession and safeguarding African children' organized by a UK-based charity, Africans United Against Child Abuse (AFRUCA). He puts,

"In fact, I had my doubts as to how far the conference could go in addressing this important topic. Because Africa is a deeply religious society, and very often faith, dogma, and tradition trump human rights whenever issues concerning Africa are discussed. Faith or better religion is at the root of most problems that plague the continent, including that of witchcraft accusation. Sadly, many Africans are reluctant to acknowledge this. Many more people in the region are unwilling to challenge religious doctrines, traditions, and practices, particularly when they conflict with reason, science, and common sense. Many Africans do not want to question or be seen to be criticizing the dogmas of witchcraft belief. They often refrain from demanding evidence or proof of witchcraft claims. Many Christians in Africa find justification for witchcraft-related abuse in the Bible, which they believe to be the literal word of God." (Igwe, 2011).

We cannot be logically correct by trying to stop people believe what they find to be true for themselves; and also, we shall be wrong if we try to force people to change their beliefs because we find them to be untrue for ourselves. What sound to be logically correct and peace-maintaining fact is the use of the 'right for freedom of belief' that every citizen possesses.

If you deeply believe that there is witchcraft or sorcery in Africa and some people in your community are witches or sorcerers, find a way to protect you against their attacks as long as you cannot prove it so that the police or the jurisdiction of your country can deal with it. You don't need to fear, shout, accuse, or fight the people you think are witches. Why? Because such actions or reactions are peace-killing. And also, the people you believe to be witches don't fear you; they don't shout at you; they are not accusing you; and are not making you a fight that can be seen by other people or the police officers. Why do you want to do for them what they never do for you if you think it is a retaliation aiming to protect yourself and the society?

The AGLR should be free from witchcraft or sorcery mentality that brings what is believed to have taken place in the invisible world to the mob jurisdiction or the state jurisdiction of the visible world. If you are spiritual to believe in the spiritual affairs, you need to deal with them in the spiritual realm to avoid any physical attacks that always impede durable peace and prosperity for all. Religious leaders should be very careful about what they teach their adepts; they should not alert people by propagating messages that communicate fear and lies. That is very important because witchcraft or sorcery mentality that prevails in the urban areas of the AGLR today has nothing to do with 'African traditions or practices' as many people may think.

Some of the practices witches and sorcerers of today are mostly measured and understood well by the religious teachings and beliefs that exist in the societies today. And those teachings have considerable consequences on people's mentalities – positive or negative – making them adopt certain ways of living which are sometimes not in harmony with good social cohabitation. After research about the 'child witch phenomena' in the capital city of the one of the countries of AGLR, the DRC, Molina (2005, p. 9) writes,

> "Our first research, in 1999, clearly showed the changes that had occurred in the mentality of Kinshasa's inhabitants. Witchcraft was perceived as fundamentally negative, unlike in the villages where witchcraft could be a positive or a negative thing. Witchcraft as we know it today has little to do with "traditional practices". It is quite clearly a modern invention, largely urban in origin, in which common cultural roots have been distorted from their primary meaning. And this is by no means something that is unique to the Congo. Revivalist church pastors, recognized as experts by the people, generally agree that witchcraft is the art of doing evil. It comes directly from Satan, assisted

by demons (or fallen angels), and stops at no despicable act in order to achieve its aims. Emphasis is placed on the unworldly aspect of witchcraft and it is described as an evil power capable of doing harm, bringing bad luck, spreading illness and killing. This power may be exercised by individuals from any social class, as well as by politicians. Some pastors give this assertion a more concrete dimension by saying that witches have a very deep sense of psychology. Some see witchcraft as just another illness that can be cured. They affirm the existence of child witches but consider that 90% of the children brought to them are not witches." (Molina, 2005).

It is reported that there are about 50,000 children living on the streets of Kinshasa, all abandoned after being accused of witchcraft (Fagge, 2015). So, if some religious leaders, the pastors, in the capital city of Kinshasa consider most of the accused children as not witches, it would be good for the whole AGLR to have religious leaders or adepts who will have the same consideration about the accused. Why? The issue is very tricky and cannot be managed well in the physical world as we mentioned in the previous paragraphs.

For example, if you cannot fight against Satan and his fallen angels by your intellectual or physical power, how dare you try to do it for the witches and sorcerers who are their simple agents? Or if you believe your God is supreme and Satan and his fallen angels are so weaker and powerless than Him, why then do you fear those who work on the account of Satan? Fear is the enemy of peace; it is the enemy of personal development toward prosperity. And when that becomes impossible for many individuals, it becomes impossible for the whole community.

As it was already mentioned early in the introduction of this book, in the AGLR, the majority of the population are Christians with about more than 85 percent and the second large religious group is Islam with about 7 percent of the total population of the region. This being the situation, we can assume that the higher majority of people in the AGLR have a spiritual belief in witchcraft or sorcery based on what the teachings of their religions convey. It is important to know that Christianity and Islam believe in witchcraft as being from and for Satan.

However, it is good to understand the reality that all the religious leaders do not have the same mindsets about witchcraft mentality in the AGLR. Some examine every correctly the accused people who come to them as shown in the quote of the previous paragraph and some others do consider all accusation as being true. While we are trying to address the issue of witchcraft mentality that is one of the barriers for durable peace and prosperity for all in the AGLR, we should be aware of the existence those religious leaders and the magical agents who work day and night to make sure that mentality continue to exist in the people's minds for their personal financial gains. These leaders create witchcraft mentality in some people's minds to make sure their businesses continue. They try to behave like artisans of peace while they are the true peace-destroyers in the communities.

Molina J. A. talks about them by showing how much some Christian churches and magical movements enjoy doing business with witchcraft mentality in the following quote.

> "It is clear that the different religious and magical movements, whether Catholic, Pentecostal, African or fetishist, fuel hatred and violence against children. Most of the churches operate on a profit-making basis and nearly all of those practicing exorcism will put on a real performance for the purposes of financial gain. What is more, and with very few exceptions, when it comes to exorcism, they tend to target "clients" and not the faithful as you might expect. These churches demonstrate the corruption of State officials, who draw clear profit from them in the form of illegal payments. On the

other hand, the churches also operate as reference points for families who have neither access to, nor confidence in, basic or social services." (Molina, 2005, p. 6).

We should not keep silence while people are being cheated by the so-called 'servants of God' and some 'fetishists' who are using lies to instigate the witchcraft mentality in the minds of 'their clients'. And unfortunately, those 'clients' believe so much in what they are told up to the extent of going to meet other people in the community to propagate the believed lies!

The other way people use of witchcraft mentality in the AGLR is through consulting witches to harm or kill others with whom they are in conflict. People who do that are very destructive by the fact that they make the community lose the people or things that were still for the development of all. They also encourage the witches who are being used to destroy or kill others to continue their dirty businesses. Kombo (2003, p. 81) talks about that by inscribing,

> "There are people who pay large sums of money to witches so that they may inflict pain or death on their enemies. The lure of money will always entice practitioners to continue with it especially because in most cases, getting caught does not bring with it fearsome retribution. The extreme poverty faced by many people will always drive them to use the relatively cheaper services of the witch to fulfill certain obligations, which would otherwise be too expensive to fulfill. For example, persons who feel wronged by others may find it difficult to pursue justice through legal means, which may involve hiring the services of a lawyer."

The witchcraft beliefs or practices in the AGLR can also weaken the cooperation between people of different regions or villages in a country. In a country like Rwanda where witchcraft is mainly associated with poison, there could be too much fear about where and how to eat or to drink when there is a need. Nobody trusts nobody when thinking about the human basic needs for survival! How can the local restaurants in a village function to make its customers feel comfortable and safe when eating and drinking? "When Rwandans say witch, they really mean someone who poisons people. Witches and poison are widely believed in throughout Rwanda, though Peace Corps staff members (especially the Rwandans) tell us that belief in poisoning is merely the result of the fear of the unknown and provincialism." (Ian in Rwanda. 3rd June 2012).

The witchcraft mentality is a dangerous illness that kills peace and prosperity, and unfortunately, it goes beyond the African continent where some Africans immigrate. It could be less dangerous if it were only limited to some tribes of the AGLR and on the regional settings only, but dwells in the minds of some people moving with it everywhere they go.

It is a pity! Let's consider the information that was given by the British Broadcast Corporation (BBC) about consequence of witchcraft mentality in London where some people from DRC were living.

> "An "obsession" with witchcraft and sorcery led a couple to brutally murder a 15-year-old boy at a flat in east London. Eric Bikubi, 28, and his partner Magalie Bamu, aged 29, have been convicted at the Old Bailey of killing Kristy Bamu after accusing him of being a sorcerer who practiced witchcraft. The couple, who live in Newham, acted after accusing Kristy of controlling and adversely influencing a young boy, the jury was told. They originally came from the Democratic Republic of Congo, where witchcraft is called Kindoki, and exorcisms are carried out in some churches. In 2010, Unicef reported 20,000 children accused of witchcraft were living on the streets of DR Congo's capital Kinshasa. In the DR Congo, accusing a child of being possessed is a criminal offense, a law that has been in place for several years. But in 2008 I traveled to Kinshasa to see if it was making any difference and, at that time, the answer was not at all. Which is why I found myself in one of the city's slums late at night

knocking on the door of tin-roofed shack that doubled as a church. Image caption A pastor had diagnosed three children as having Kindoki. Pastor Tsimba let me in and showed me three children who he had diagnosed as having Kindoki. The youngest was probably six, the oldest no more than 12. They had been in the church for days, deprived of food and forced to work. Their parents were paying for the privilege. The only light came from flickering candles and storm lamps. The pastor began to shout and pray." (Crawnford, 2012).

Atrocious acts due to witchcraft beliefs and practices also take place in other countries of the AGLR. For example in Uganda children are sometimes kidnapped to be used as sacrifices by witch-doctors. Some look some parts of their bodies by the same phenomena. Allan Brian Senyoga (2010) had also noticed the peace-troubling acts of witchcraft mentality in the AGLR; he writes,

> "In Uganda stories of child sacrifice have reached an all-time high and no longer even make it to the front page. Children are kidnapped and sacrificed by witch-doctors on a regular basis. Parents are now compelled to have their young children's ears pierced at the earliest opportunity as such kids are considered unsuitable for sacrifice."

In the same country Uganda, the media had reported that graves of the victims of Rwandan Genocide of 1994 have been used by witches? Why? Is it to have power in the witchcraft activities to harm or kill more people in the AGLR? Or to make the lives of the people who remain alive more and more better? Witchcraft mentality or the witchcraft beliefs and practices in Africa will never improve the lives of people although many Africans will not agree with reality. Instead, with such mentality withes are just using the remains of the dead people to have more people dead! It is just the use of the victims of Genocide to create victims of witchcraft! A loss that is used to create a loss; and what will be the future of the AGLR.

On 23 March 2009, the media 'Mail & Guardians' (2009) reported "A report has found that the remains of genocide victims buried in mass graves in Uganda have been exhumed to be used in witchcraft. A report by Rwanda's Parliament has found that the remains of genocide victims buried in mass graves in Uganda have been exhumed to be used in witchcraft ceremonies, Rwandan media reported. The *New Times*, citing a copy of the report, said one mass grave in Masaka District, in central Uganda, was tampered with and many bodies washed away downriver. "At the mass grave in Masaka District we found a bottle of local brew, coins and other witchcraft materials on top of the grave," the report said. "This clearly indicates that the bodies are exhumed and possibly used for witchcraft purposes." The parliamentary report comes at a sensitive time, with the 15th anniversary of the beginning of the genocide fast approaching."

The very negative reality about people with witchcraft mentality (both accused and accuser) is that they move everywhere with it. Their mindsets about witchcraft do not change with a simple change of location. They seem to be tied to it; therefore they become mentally paralyzed or enslaved about their witchcraft beliefs or practices. They cannot in true peace with themselves and other almost everywhere they go because of the power of their witchcraft beliefs or practices. That is why they are permanent agents who can easily put peace in trouble in the community. That is why in the capitals of the countries of the AGLR there are many accused children who are being parented by the streets! These children in the streets are a permanent threat to the security of people in urban areas because of their psychological states that make them 'ready to harm, still, or kill.'

So, all the parents and any other adult of the AGLR need to understand this reality and hate it in order to be able to change or to teach others for a positive change of mentality concerning witchcraft beliefs and practices. If that is done, then the children of the region will also have a good and positive mind about that; and all the communities will be safe from the atrocities that come from witchcraft or sorcery activities or beliefs.

7.2.6. Natural Resources Mismanagement Mentality (NRMM)

"If we are to remain free, if we are to enjoy the full benefit
of Africa's resources, we must be united to plan for our
total defense and the full exploitation of our
material and human means in the full
interest of all our people.
To go it alone will limit our horizons, curtail our
expectations and threaten our liberty."
(Kwame Nkrumah)

What is Natural Resources Mismanagement Mentality (NRMM) in the AGLR?

'Natural Resource Mismanagement Mentality (NRMM) is the attitude or mindsets of some people in the AGLR that push them to violate the natural principles that govern any good management of natural resources for their egoistic benefits instead of those of all in the community, in the country, in the African continent, in the world. For example, in the context of the AGLR, the lack of moral virtues like fairness, free-giving, sharing, care-taking, incorruptibleness, emptiness, etc. can be considered as symptoms or signs of natural resources mismanagement mentality.

Because natural resources exist to serve the needs of natural beings without barriers, people with such mentality try to stop or to sicken the normal flow of what should naturally serve everybody in the community. On this point, we need to be specific about what we are talking about due to the broadness of the concept of 'natural resources'.

So, during the next paragraphs concerning this section, after going through some characteristics of people with 'Natural Resource Mismanagement Mentality', we are going to focus on the impact of that mentality in the AGLR with facts and comments made mainly on land resources, water resources, energy resources, food resources (agriculture), soil resources, and mineral resources.

Characteristics of Natural Resources Mismanagement Mentality in the AGLR

People with 'Natural Resource Mismanagement Mentality' seem to exhibit several of negative characteristics that can match the following list but not limited to it.

- They seem to be ignorant of the natural relationship that exists between the human beings and other beings (trees for examples); that is how they behave regardless the level of their formal education (even when having university or college degrees).

- They are ready to sacrifice people for the sake of resources and fail to make wise use of it (useless spending for example).

- They don't protect the environment (for example, they cut trees without planting other).

- They don't care about rare species (in animal kingdoms, vegetation, etc.).

- They seem to be difficult to teach or advise in terms of environment protection (they seem to means: God will provide more!).

- Etc.

Impact of Natural Resources Mismanagement Mentality in the AGLR: does it really hinder durable peace and prosperity in AGLR

Obviously, it can be astonishing and alarming to learn that some people are dying from curable diseases and hunger and get buried in a very rich land that contains some of the rarest minerals in the world and the richest natural resources of diverse categories. It does not sound fair to have been born in a very naturally rich village and die from poverty and suffering caused by fake leaders of the country who are corrupted or take by force for themselves what belong to all the villagers, or by bullets resulting from the fight of militias who want to plunder the natural resources that exist for the prosperity of all for themselves. Why has that been happening? The answer to this question is the 'Natural Resource Mismanagement Mentality' in the minds of some African leaders in the AGLR.

In fact, in the press release of Africa Progress Panel (nd) we find the following important thought-provoking questions of Kofi Annan, the former General Secretary of the UN and president of the Africa Progress Panel: "But it is time to ask why so much growth has done so little to lift people out of poverty – and why so much of Africa's resource wealth is squandered through corrupt practices and unscrupulous investment activities." He also puts "Africa is a continent of great wealth so why is Africa's share of global malnutrition and child deaths rising so fast? The answer is that inequality is weakening the link between economic growth and improvements in well-being."

Challender at al. (2003, p.3) deplore the mismanagement mentality of some leaders of developing countries in the following quote,

> "Oil, gas and mining can generate enormous wealth. Yet countries rich in minerals tend to be blighted by corruption, conflict, poor economic growth, low public spending, poor rights records and low levels of child welfare. As Save the Children has seen in the developing countries in which it works, the results of this 'resource curse' can be devastating. Where unaccountable elites divert resources for private gain, negligible investment in basic services such as health, education and sanitation results in infant deaths from easily treatable illnesses such as diarrhea."

Many analysts of the African problems, taking into account the statistics of African countries, think that there is a resource curse on Africa. A curse or a mismanagement mentality? If we believe that durable peace and prosperity for all need positive change; and if we accept to be ready for change, we need to know what must be changed for the well-being of everybody in our communities. Because, it is not a secret that "Human development performance in many resource-rich African states remains dismal. African oil and mineral exporters routinely rank near the bottom of UNDP's Human Development Index and exhibit highly inequitable levels of income and wealth." (Mailey, 2015, p. 5).

The situation is very revolting because of the pity-provoking statistics published by non-governmental organizations.

> "Statistics provide strong evidence that there is a resource curse in Africa. Many of the 20 countries in sub-Saharan Africa identified by the IMF as resource-rich countries languish toward the bottom of the Human Development Index and have some of the world's highest child mortality rates. For example, 12 African resource-rich countries have more than 100 child deaths for every 1,000 live births. The 2013 Resource Governance Index by the Revenue Watch Institute evaluates the resource governance of the oil, gas and mining sector of 58 countries globally, and finds that 16 out of 21 African countries surveyed received a "weak" or "failing" score" (SAFPI, 2013).

Is it a shame to be an African? No. The time for revolutionary change has come. And Thomas Isidore Noël Sankara, former President of Burkina Faso (1983 – 1987) and pan-Africanist theorist, also said "Never be shamed of being Afrikan". It is clear that people with 'natural resource mismanagement mentality' are shaming us for being Africans by the results of their acts, but we shall not lose our courage to fight against their inhuman acts. We shall remain proud of our African identities. A press release mentioned that "Africa's rich natural resources offer a unique opportunity for a breakthrough in improving the lives of Africa's citizens, says a major new report launched today by Kofi Annan, the former UN Secretary-General, but too often these resources are plundered by corrupt officials and foreign investors. Rising inequality is also blocking Africa from seizing that

opportunity, the report shows." Africa Progress Panel –
Press Release (nd).

How then can we try to be silent when we know that some people are plundering what was supposed to serve the general interests of the population? How can we try to be shaped by robbers and liars? We need to stand up and make a continual and non-violent fight against those who are imposing us the life of misery until social justice is totally established. We should not continue to suffer while we are supposed to enjoy the riches that are buried in our lovely African land.

All Africans and non-Africans of good will, let us unite to preach positive change of mentality to people who are mismanaging the natural resources that we all need to live well. We should unite to fight non-violently against those who will not accept to be taught for positive change; to fight against those who are forbidding us from having access to our natural resources equitably and without suffering. To fight against those who are destroying the forests that make human lives livable on the planet earth.

The United States Institute of Peace (USIP, p.3) puts it clear that "in many areas around the world, access to natural resources cannot be taken for granted. According to the United Nations, many women walk several hours a day just to find water; and more than two million people, most of them children, die from diseases associated with water stresses each year." We have to recognize that as long as most leaders in the developing countries have not changed their minds completely for the general interested of their citizens, the tragic deaths due to the resources that are available for all will always continue to happen mostly in the AGLR.

USIP (nd, p.3) also mentions that "Some experts are predicting that the world's supply of oil will run out in the not too distant future. And almost half of our old growth forests have been destroyed." Nonetheless, we should not panic and think that nothing can be done to solve the problem in the AGLR. There will be much hope for the future if there is considerable and progressive change of mentality in the population presently. In terms of minerals, if some naturally rich countries of West were able to totally improve their standards of living why not us?

Challender at al. (2003, p.8) talk about that by inscribing,

> "Mineral resources can bring enormous benefits to a country and its people. The key lies in good governance in the public interest. Mineral resource-rich countries that have become growth 'winners'

include Canada, Australia and Norway. In 1900, Norway was Europe's poorest country – in the space of a century, it has become one of the richest, and sits at the top of the UNDP's Human Development Index. Children in Norway enjoy some of the highest standards of living in the world, with a life expectancy at birth of 78.5 years and an infant mortality rate of just 4 per 1000 births."

As it is known the AGLR (DRC, Uganda, Burundi, Rwanda) is very rich in terms of natural resources and the economy of their states depends primarily on that. But how naturally rich is the AGLR compared to the other regions of Africa and the rest of the world? Can it natural resources achieve the prosperity for all if well managed? How is the AGLR naturally blessed to be able to sustain people's lives when its citizens especially the leaders work without 'Natural Resources Mismanagement Mentality'?

The geography and geology clearly shows that there can be enough for the people of the AGLR to live better lives in their respective countries. For example, the DRC is richly blessed with an estimated US$24 trillion worth of untapped deposits of raw minerals that is equivalent to the combined GDP of Europe and the US.; it has the world's largest reserves of cobalt. There are important quantity of diamonds, gold, coltan, copper, tin, etc. The country has more than 50 types of minerals identified but never exploited since the arrival of European explorers.

The DRC had the half of the African forests and the water resources; with a number of hydroelectric dams located on the Congo River in Inga, the country is able to supply electrical energy to all African countries with a surplus that can be used by Europe. The electrical potentiality of Grand Inga Dam is estimated to be so powerful with the capacity of giving an output of about 44,000 MW which can make it become the world's largest electricity-supplying dam upon completed – if the project is completed – (generating more power than three Gorges Dam in China).

The DRC has a very rich forest of about 700,000 square miles that represents about one-fifth of the world's closed-canopy tropical forest. It has over 10,000 species of plants, 1,000 species of birds, 4000 species of mammals, and three of the world's four species of great apes. All these natural resources exist in DRC but millions of people are living in a non-describable poverty and many are those who die from it.

Dilva (2013) writes "In countries such as the Democratic Republic of Congo (DRC) and Angola, which are blessed with enormous rich mineral resources many will struggle to properly describe the living conditions of the majority of their people there. Scandalous? despicable?" But you will hear politicians say that they are working for the good of the citizens. They make people think the problem of DRC and the whole African continent is related to the lack of resources. That is to keep people in eternal ignorance. Thomas Isidore Noël Sankara once said, "The enemies of a people are those who keep them in ignorance."

Moreover, the above-mentioned natural resources in the DRC do not benefit its population because they are mismanaged. "With half of Africa's forests and water resources and trillion-dollar mineral reserves, the Democratic Republic of Congo (DRC) could become a powerhouse of Africa development proved multiple pressures on its natural resources are urgently addressed." (UNEP, 2011). But why is it not so after more than 50 years of independence?

We need to address the shocking situation of this country with much stress because all its citizens should be aware of their individual responsibility to positively influence the durable peace and prosperity for the whole Africa. There is a permanent need of change of mentality regarding how people manage the natural resources available in the country. UNEP Study Confirms DR Congo's Potential as Environmental Powerhouse but Warns of Critical Threats. The United Nation Environment Program (UNEP, 2011) "warns of alarming trends including increased deforestation, species depletion, heavy metal pollution and land degradation from mining, as well as an acute drinking water crisis which has left an estimated 51 million Congolese without access to potable water."

Is this country managed by people whose consciousnesses function well? Is it fair for a huge and rich country with half of all the water of African continent having millions of people who cannot access potable water? That is one of unwanted consequences of NRMM in the minds of some Congolese leaders, especially political ones.

From the UNEP two-year environmental study conducted in cooperation with the Congolese Ministry of Education, we can find the following information related to the degradation, plunder, and misuse of the natural resources of DRC. UNEP, findings show that the DRC has the highest level of biodiversity in Africa, yet 190 species are classified as critically endangered or vulnerable on the IUCN Red List of Threatened Species. Elephants and mountain gorillas are among the species under threat (UNEP, 2011).

This situation will always be a threat to durable peace and prosperity for all in the DRC and in the whole African Great Lakes Region if people will not accept a total change of mentality. Why? Because the biodiversity of the DRC is destroyed by some Congolese and some people of the neighboring countries; and those destroyers seem to ignore that what belongs to the DRC is also for the whole AGLR, the whole African Continent, the whole world.

The UN Experts report of 2015 mentions the vast and uncontrolled illegal exploitation of wildlife in DRC has a major impact on the abundance of biodiversity of the country. The report gives an estimation of 22,000-25,000 elephants killed in Africa every year by poachers and less than 2,500 elephants are killed in the DRC. It puts that the ivory that is traded is generally shipped west through the

DRC province of Kisangani, east through Bunia, and south through Beni and Butembo; and some ivory have been transported by plane or helicopter including to South Sudan and Uganda (UNEP-MONUSCO-OSESG, 2015).

The figures showing loss in terms of animal population in the DRC are considerable. We need to address this issue with much concern because the naturally richest part of Africa is being made the poorest one. For example, in the National Park Garamba, the annual losses stated in the next passage is eloquent to show us how much the AGLR is losing what exist to sustain the lives of its people.

> "In Garamba National Park the confirmed poaching in 2012 was 40 elephants, and in the first nine months of 2013 16 elephants. In 2014 at least 131 elephants were poached in Garamba. While ivory poaching may have played a larger role to some groups, the elephant populations within the provinces of Maniema, North and South Kivu and Orientale are so heavily reduced in numbers that their role as threat finance or strategic control is at

best   peripheral   now."   (UNEP-MONUSCO-OSESG, 2015, p.11).

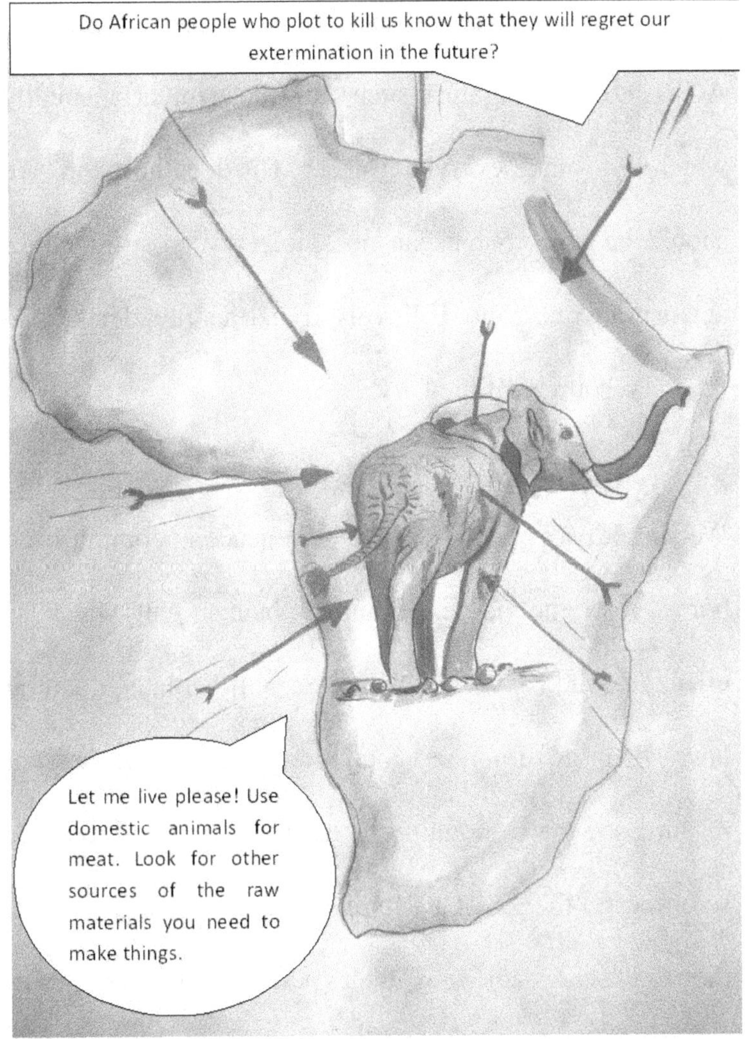

Any person of good will or any patriot will agree with me that we should do all our best to mobilize the people of AGRL to fight against such mismanagement mentality which will make everybody loser if it does not stop. We should be able to make a non-violent very strong fight against anyone who is involved in the plunder of the natural resources of the DRC.

We should work hard to make sure peace is coming back home. And the peace of human beings will never be effective when some of them are still violating natural laws that govern the good management of natural resources. So, we should work hard hand in hand to make sure trees in the forest are living there in peace, animals in the forest are enjoying their peace, and every other creatures that makes the components of our very rich biodiversity. If we succeed to do that, the result will be positive because we have to understand well the inviolable relationship between the lives of human beings on planet earth and the lives of forests or bushes (trees, animals, etc.).

Maybe we also need to teach the course of 'civil education' and the importance of wild animal for the sector of tourism of a country to Congolese people who are involved in the illicit sells of wild animals. Maybe we also need to teach the same course to the political leaders who are leading the country today reminding them the importancs of making sure the forests are safe.

It is so regrettable to see that no one is there to protect the wild animal populations because "With a price range of USD 150-400 per kg and ten kg of ivory per elephant on average, the gross value of ivory to criminal armed groups amounts to ca. 2,565-3,065 killed elephants per year or 25.7-30.64 tons of ivory, giving a possible maximum range of ivory as threat finance to all African non-state armed groups of ca. UDS four-12,2 million, dependent upon their ability to strike elephant populations at greater distances." (UNEP-MONUSCO-OSESG, 2015, p.11).

Millions of dollars in the pockets of robbers are now important than thousands of elephants in the forests that are able to generate more than that without being killed and for the interest of all the citizens of the country. What kind of national loss? Yes, the nation is losing but the plunders should remember that there is nothing for nothing. That is the natural laws that appear to be unbreakable.

People go everywhere with the wrong acts that they have done, and they cannot have inner peace. That is why we are putting stress on positive change of mentality in order to regain inner peace. And once you have regained your inner peace, you will be able to welcome the principles that will help you to effectively contribute to the establishment of durable peace and prosperity for all. Because the elephants that you are systematically plundering do not belong to you, they belong to the whole nation – and to the whole world.

The UN Experts report of April 2015 states "40. Indeed, less than 100 elephants are killed by non-state armed groups in eastern DRC every year, simply because there are so few elephants left. Using estimates from UNEP-INTERPOL and local sources, with an average of 1.8 tusks per elephant and 5.5 kg per tusk and a local price of

USD 70-400 per kg, then the possible maximum income is only 70,000-400,000 USD per year for local non-state armed groups." (UNEP-MONUSCO-OSESG, 2015, p.12). Can you image fire weapons are manufactured mainly outside Africa, and then they are supplied to Africans to destroy themselves by killing each other and deteriorating their biodiversity?

UNEP (2011) also document that "Up to 1.7 million tones of bush-meat (mainly antelope, duiker, monkey and wild board) are harvested annually from unregulated hunting and poaching, contribution to species depletion." Do the people in the DRC lack 'green spaces' or pasturage for domestic animal breeding to avoid using wild animal as meat for their daily meals? What kind of mentality is that? How can people keep on destroying the beings that constitute important source of funds for the country?

Obviously, no tourist can go in the AGLR or in the DRC to just visit cows or goats. But if they can go there to visit antelopes, monkey, etc. Also, it is practically easy and less risky to live on domestic meats through breeding rather than going to hunt in forests. It might be that the people who are killing wild animals for meats in the DRC are the illegal gun holders or the rebel militias. But, they can rear domestic animals where they are living. If they claim to be fighting against injustice and mismanagement of the politicians in the government, why are they destroying what constitute the richness of the state while they were supposed to protect them?

People who are involved in those activities need to accept positive change of mentality that will be an important contribution to durable peace and prosperity for all.

Change is not difficult or impossible; it is part of human beings' lives on the planet earth. Julius Nyerere, former President of Tanzania, puts "Change has, throughout history, been a constant part of human experience. But today change is more rapid than ever before; its implications are very comprehensive, and yet its first approach is often imperceptible." (Mwakikagile, 2006).

For example, the 'powerful oxygen factory' generated by the big forest of DRC is not used only by Congolese, it is the whole AGLR that uses it, it is the whole world that uses it. If trees are massively cut without replanting many more in the DRC, it is the whole AGLR that is losing but I wonder why the members of the transnational plunder system do not realize that.

> "The DRC's tropical rain forests extend over 1.55 million km^2 and account for more than half of Africa's forest resources – making them a critical global ecosystem service provider and a potential

source of up to US$900 million in annual revenue up to 2030 through REDD+." (UNEP, 2011).

But are these millions of dollars generated for the prosperity of all in the RDC? No. Why? The leadership problem due to 'Natural Resource Mismanagement Mentality' will always make the country lose if people do not change positively. This mismanagement mentality for leaders is more dangerous than a mortal illness in the body of an individual; because a sick person may die alone but people with that mentality are likely to kill millions of people by poverty, ignorance, diseases, wars, and genocide. The resources are there, but no leaders are working to make sure they are adequately exploited for the good of all the citizens.

As we mentioned in the paragraph above, the rich natural resources of the DRC are not supposed to benefit the Congolese only, they exist for the good of everybody in

Africa, in the world. How? Although the foreigners are not supposed to be the primary beneficiaries of the natural resources of the DRC, but they cannot be excluded from taking advantage from them even if they are excellently managed.

For example, the waters of the rivers of the Congo basin flow to the neighboring countries, the oxygen produced by the trees of the huge forest of DRC is used both Congolese and by citizens of the neighboring of DRC, and the good management of natural resources of the country will not stop that! This is just to consider the natural flow of natural resources as God intended to be without any involvement of human activities such as regional and international trade based on natural resources being another form that foreigners may benefit from riches of DRC.

The point here is to show that the natural resources of DRC should be managed well for the well-being of Congolese first and for the well-being of the AGLR, the whole Africa, and the whole World. DRC exists on the planet earth and its huge natural resources potential cannot be for other planets. So, their mismanagement will surely have negative impact on the whole planet earth. When international and national organizations reports of forest deterioration and land degradation and population in DRC, some people may think that the consequences are for Congolese only; of course the country will be the first loser, but it's the planet earth is being negatively affected too, it is being put under progressive degradation too.

And the irony of the situation is that some African leaders who are taking part in that are being praised by some other people of being 'good leaders!' UNEP (2011) reported that "The RDC has the largest artisanal mining workforce in the world – around two million people – but a lack of controls have led to land degradation and pollution. Its untapped minerals reserves are of global importance and are estimated to be worth US$24 trillion." Why does the mining sector of the DRC lack control?

Is it not peace and prosperity killing attitude a government to fail to initiate efficient organizations that can generate enough funds to fight against poverty with effective controls over them and the people who are working in the whole mining sector of the country? How can a government say that they do not have enough funds to run the state projects and institutions while they are not able to control the sources of finances that they already have? What kind of mentality is that?

The 'Natural Resource Mismanagement Mentality' will always be a strong barrier to durable peace and prosperity for all in the countries that depend primarily on natural resources as a source of funds to run the state institutions. That is why we can assume that if people change positively in the AGLR, the whole political and economic system of the region will change for the common good of all. If that does not happen national peace-troubling issues will persist because the AGLR has what the world needs to run many of its companies. And those companies seem to be ready to get what they need by any means! And most of that is located in the DRC.

That is why there are so many civilians victims there, particularly the children.

> "With vast deposits of coltan, a key mineral used in mobile telephones and information technology, the

Democratic Republic of Congo (DRC) is in the grip of conflict, and infant mortality rates in parts of eastern DRC reached a terrible 41 per cent per year in 2001. Save the Children estimates that oil, gas and mining industries are important in over 50 developing countries which are home to some 3.5 billion people. One and a half billion of these people, including at least 700 million children, live on less than $2 a day." (Challender, C. at al., 2003, p.3).

What kind of unfairness in the developing countries of the world? What kind of unfairness in the AGLR? What kind of unfairness in the DRC? If the minerals and other types of natural resources cannot be used to sustain the lives of the citizens, for what reason do they exist now? If they are used to kill millions of people, why should they be exploited? Is it their buyers who tell the leaders of AGLR do misuse the funds that they get from the sell?

Are the African leaders forced to still the money from their states and go to keep them in western financial institutions and other organizations while their people are lacking foods, medicines, and other basic needs for their daily lives? Who are these people who cannot feel pity for the millions of children who are dying in Africa and in their personal countries while they are shipping millions of stolen dollars for safe-keeping in some western countries? What destiny and happiness do those leaders believe to have with the mentality of sending young people, women, and babies to the world of their ancestors using famine and forced labor as their strongest weapon? Is it impossible for the buyers of the minerals to get what they need without deaths of human beings, trees, animals, and other rare plants in the DRC?

Any human heart and spirit free from diseases may feel very sorry for the innocent people who have been losing their lives in the AGLR. It is reported,

> "Over 2.5 million people have died since the outbreak of war, many of them children. A joint

report by Save the Children, Oxfam and Christian Aid found women and children to have borne a disproportionate burden of suffering in emergency situations engendered by the conflict. Many children have been separated from their families and infant mortality rates in parts of eastern DRC reached a horrifying 41 percent per year in 2001." (Challender, C. at al., 2003, p.20)

That is the work of people with natural resource mismanagement mentality, of people without correct destiny, of people who think they are eternal on this planet earth. This is a seemingly imposed fate of the people of a country that is said can be the 'economic engine' of the whole Africa with "Around 15 tonnes of mercury are used annually artisanal gold mining operations, making it the second largest source of mercury emissions in Africa." (UNEP, 2011). As it is clearly reported, the AGLR is naturally powerful to transform Africa into a prosperous continent; but instead of doing that, the leaders and some other individuals of the region are using the available natural power to destroy the lives of millions.

Moreover, the destruction of human lives in the AGLR is generalized for touching all the areas of life in the region. This means that people are not being tormented or killed by gun-bullets only; but also ignorance, lack of medicine, hunger as mentioned in the previous paragraphs of this section. For example, Food penitential is higher in the DRC than other countries of the AGRL but foreign countries seem to benefit from that than the Congolese Citizens.

It is reported that "the Congo basin supports Africa's largest inland fisheries with an estimated production potential of 520,000 tonnes per year. While at the national level this resource is under-exploited, there are many instances of serious over-fishing pressures at the local level." This is also one of the negative results of natural resource mismanagement mentality in the DRC. Some of the political leaders spend much time talking too much and do nothing to positively change their own minds to be able to manifest constructive acts that can eradicate poverty of the masses.

It is so revolting to see foreigners or neighboring countries taking advantage of what could help the nationals because their leaders are unable to use them adequately to make better the national economic health of their countries. Positive change is really needed; we need to accept it and to vulgarize it in all the communities of the AGLR to fight against the ignorance of the masses who are always victims of natural resource mismanagement mentality.

Also, it is a pity to see the suffering of the masses who are left in total darkness by their leaders. Colonized people of the neocolonialism, they are made unable to live well by the people they vote to lead them! What ingratitude of the voted leaders? 'Dear political leaders', how can you increase the misery and poverty of the people who elected you to serve them? Are you different from a person who cut the breasts of a woman who breastfed him or her? The following illustration shows how that the political leaders who do not work to serve the interest of the citizens of the countries of AGLR and who mismanage the natural resources of their countries to serve their egoistic interest instead of those of the masses they are supposed to work for are not so different from a person who cut the breasts his or her mother.

That is why the minds of many people in the AGLR need to be healed of natural resource mismanagement mentality (NRMM) because if it does not stop, the situation will be more disastrous in the future than today. Even the rain that is abundant in the AGLR will become rare if people refuse to positively change the NRMM to manage well the natural resources of the region. The report of UNEP (2011) mentions "The most alarming climate change-related issue is the vulnerability of rain-fed small-scale agriculture.

For example, as of 2020, the duration of the rainy season in the drought-prone region of Katanga is expected to reduce from seven months to five months." If this is estimated to happen in one of the provinces of DRC, what about its neighboring countries like Rwanda, Burundi, etc. where there are less forest trees and waters? On the facts concerning the NRMM, you can notice that much stress is put on the DRC. The reason is that the DRC plays a very important role in understanding most wars and rebel movements of the AGRL.

Moreover, the DRC is a country that has numbered several rebel movements reported to have been supported by some neighboring countries because of its rich natural resources. It is a country that produces almost all the oxygen that the people of the AGLR need to survive! To show the importance of the natural resources of DRC, UNEP (2011) report puts,

> "There is a remarkable rise of 'people-based' social enterprises, most of which rely on natural resources. Yet with a fragile banking system and limited incentives to formalize transactions, the formal sector's growth has become a critical structural problem as businesses can operate beyond environmental and labor laws."

People rely on the natural resources to do business but they are not doing it with good moral virtues and effective management skills. Some may wonder how do we know that? The situation of the lives of citizens shows clearly how badly the natural resources are managed. Even reports of NGOs put it clear that DRC lacks good leaders and managers that can adequately contribute to the process of establishing durable peace and prosperity for all by managing well the natural resources of the country.

For example, it is very regrettable to learn that the people of the DRC are still lacking access to necessary basic services like energy and water while the environment of the country is naturally blessed to supply that to every Congolese and to the rest of Africa and world. We read that "As it is still emerging from a long period of State decline and protracted crises, the provision of basic services, including energy and water supply, and environmental problems in urban centers remain key challenges for the DRC." (UNEP, 2011).

Can you image a huge and natural rich country in the AGLR with almost all the waters of the continent but where there is scarcity of water and energy in places where "Fewer than 40% of the nearly 70 million inhabitants live in urban areas, according to the latest NSI (National Statistics Institute) estimates (World Bank, 2015, DRC Country Overview). So, if those services lack in the urban areas what about the rural ones where most people live? This is the time for the DRC to have leaders who are healed from NRMM. It is time to have people who will not make the shame of AGLR; it is time to stand up for a positive change of mentality to welcome durable peace and prosperity for all.

It is time to refuse to die from hunger while the AGLR millions of hectares of arable land that are not exploited. It is time to deny dying in poverty while the AGLR has a country with many minerals that can boost the economy of the whole African Continent if well managed. Is it not an unacceptable situation to suffer poverty and hunger in a country with competitive natural potentials?

"With 80 million hectares of arable land and over 1,100 minerals and precious metals, the DRC has the potential to be one of the richest countries on the African continent and a driver of African growth." (World Bank, 2015, DRC Country Overview). And with that, political leaders of DRC seem to have no idea of what to do to stop or reduce their deep dependence on foreign aids to run the government and other state institutions!

That is why people need to read carefully this book to know what are the exact problems and what solutions are durable for the AGRL to have durable peace and prosperity for all. The time for international and national lies should be over because it seems embarrassing to learn that in order "to support the DRC's development challenges, a doubling of aid is urgently needed, including an estimated US$200 million per annum for the environment." (UNEP, 2011).

However, some people with the NRMM in the DRC have been helped by some neighboring foreign countries to plunder the natural resources of the country in detriment of the national interests of the citizens. Countries like Rwanda, Uganda, Burundi, and Zimbabwe have been reported to have been involved in the pillage of natural resources of DRC. How did they do it while they are foreign countries? They were surely facilitated to do that by some Congolese soldiers and civilians ready to kill their own brothers and sisters to enrich themselves.

Challender, C. at al. (2003, p.20) talks about that situation showing how the conflicts in the AGLR were created by national and foreign plunders of natural resources of DRC. He puts,

> "While Congolese forces are by no means without blame, it is to a large degree foreign armed forces that have plundered the DRC's mineral resources during the war, especially those of Rwanda, Uganda and Zimbabwe. The November 2002 report of the UK All Party Parliamentary Group (APPG) on the Great Lakes and Genocide Prevention draws on clear evidence that foreign armies have deliberately waged war in order to carry out this exploitation. For instance, the report points to how the Zimbabwean regime has used its presence to initiate advantageous joint business ventures with the DRC Government and companies in order to exploit some of the most precious resources. Similarly, in eastern DRC, 'opportunistic' Ugandan generals have decentralized power enabling them to establish Ugandan or Congolese-led companies. Rwandan

politicians and army officers have either directly exploited mineral resources themselves or secured favorable terms by which Rwandan-owned companies can do the same."

It could be argued that it's the group of organized armed plunders who are never happy when there is no conflict in the AGRL. Can you imagine a situation in which a cunning person putting two parties into conflict so that they may fight to be divided by what is supposed to unite them? Study the following illustration to find out how cunning the plunders are; they put people into conflict so that they may still what could make them become prosperous if well managed.

Some people with NRMM have been always working with international companies to help them achieve their destructive aim: becoming rich by mismanagement of natural resources of the country. "It should also be noted that there are a number of companies involved in the illegal exploitation of natural resources that fall under government jurisdiction in developed countries.

In 2002, a UN panel of experts listed 84 international companies working in the DRC that are considered to be in violation of the OECD Guidelines for Multinational Enterprises (Challender, C. at al., 2003, p.21). Those companies seem to work hard to make sure rebel movements will not end because they are getting what they need (raw materials) at a very cheap price and the expense of to Congolese human sweat and blood! The well-organized armed groups work hand in hand with those companies to continue their bloody businesses that have cost the lives of millions of people in the DRC. And the rebel leaders of the armed groups, Congolese or not, take advantage of the revenue they receive from those companies in their corroborated illegal natural resources exploitation. Is it a win-win situation? No, one part is scandalously loosing but the hunger for riches and the ignorance of the truth have blinded them. The UN Exports report of April 2015 puts,

> "9. Revenue from illegal natural resources exploitation finances a high number of well over 25 armed groups (up to 49 according to some estimates) continuing to destabilize eastern DRC. While the armed groups have their own proven survival strategies, transnational organized crime networks might try to 'divide and rule' armed groups in eastern DRC to prevent any single armed group from achieving a dominant role and potentially interfering with illegal exploitation rackets run by transnational criminal networks." (UNEP-MONUSCO-OSESG, 2015, p.4)

How sly are the companies of plunders? Should we keep silence while those people are freely killing innocent in order to still? Are the millions of dollars worthier than the lives of millions of people? Mailey (2015, p.6) also inscribes "Natural resource wealth has also been intimately linked to violent conflict across Africa. In the Democratic Republic of the Congo, rebel groups have used the proceeds of mineral sales to fund their military operations." (Mailey, 2015, p. 6). This is so crazy to think about. Using people's natural resources to kill them! What exaggerated unfairness is that?

And it is lamentable to learn that the neighboring like Rwanda, Burundi, and Uganda may be used by the transnational networks of criminal robbers to achieve their inhuman acts. If these neighbors think they are profiting from that, they are not smart. There is not profit you can have from robbing neighbors because their warmth will always be attending to your home and their coldness too. The UN Experts report of April 2015 mentions "The majority minerals mined in the DRC are the 3Ts – cassiterite (tin), wolframite (tungsten), coltan (tantalum) –

gold, diamonds, cobalt and copper. Minerals fare smuggled across borders to Rwanda, Burundi, and Uganda as well as in other parts of DRC." (UNEP – MONUSCO – OSESG, 2015, p.8).

The key findings of the report published on April, 15th 2015 by the UN experts on illegal exploitation and trade of natural resources of DRC are alarming. Some victims of what have been happening in the AGLR especially in the DRC can either be shocked or disturbed by the reports that put clear some of the raisons d'être of rebel movements and militias claiming to exist for the good of the citizens.

The report of the experts shows that the illicit natural resources exploitation in eastern DRC is at over USD 1.25 billion per year according to some estimates and of about USD 722-862 million if excluding diamonds which is also sourced outside eastern DRC. And of these amounts about 72-426 million per annum (estimated 10-30 per cent) goes to transnational organized criminal groups (UNEP-MONUSCO-OSESG, 2015). That is the cost of the lives of millions of people in the AGLR. While Africa is crying the lost of its millions of people since colonization up to nowadays, some Africans with NRMM continue to increase the death toll! Are they really benefiting?

Now, are the people involved in the plunder taking conscience that they will not enjoy the wealth they dishonestly get for eternity? Do those mis-managers realize that their lives on this planet earth are soon ending and they will join the millions of people they innocently killed? Maybe they don't have time to think of what they are doing! But the time has come to make them think of what they have been doing. It is time for every African of the AGLR to be aware of their destructive games by refusing to be victimized by people with dirty minds, by who are always ready to kill their own brothers and sisters to get riches.

A positive change of mentality should occur in the AGLR, if not millions of innocent civilians will continue to be victim of the cruel system of plunders using guns. Everybody needs to be aware of what has been happening in the AGRL because we all need positive changes followed by positive actions. The situation is so critical in the region because of the double loss (humans and natural resources); the organized criminals are making huge money in detriment to the citizens who are supposed to enjoy the riches of their countries.

I think we have made good business last time. Haven't we? Now, you don't need to doubt about my credibility. I see that your 'troops' have made a great job. Are all these sacs full of coltan only or there are other minerals inside? Should I give you dollars and guns as last time? Or you only need dollars?
Yes boss. Last time it was okay. Today, we only need money. You are still having enough guns and bullets to use. The coltan you see here is of very good quality; we are going to increase the price of a kilogram... I know you will enjoy them in your company especially when making electronic devices like computers. And I will also be happy to use a computer that will be made of this mineral because of its quality!!!

For example, the report of the UN experts mentions that the organized criminal groups get estimated annual net profits of USD 40-120 million from gold, USD 16-48 million from timber, USD 12-35 million from charcoal, USD 7.5-22.6 million from 3T minerals, USD 16-48 million from diamonds sourced mainly from outside the conflict zone, USD 14.3-28 million from other natural resources like wildlife, ivory, fisheries, etc. (UNEP-MONUSCO-OSESG, 2015).

The fishing sector is also mismanaged by both the leaders in the governments and the leaders of rebel movements. The information about that is not documented enough, but some findings concerning that in the DRC may shed light to help understand what is happening in the fishing sector of the country. We need to ask why the government authorities keep on asking aids from outside the country while they are not even able to manage well what they already have!

Does it sound logical for the leaders of the country to ask for more money while they are unable to just supervise the existing economic activities done mainly on the exploitation of natural resources to gain revenue for the state? Is it not silly to look for what you need outside your home while they are already located there? I have to humbly and honestly express my opinion that the countries of AGRL, particularly the DRC, do not primarily need foreign aids to build durable peace and prosperity for all. They just need good managerial skills and excellent moral virtues built on the good principles of nationalism; they need a positive change of mentality because if they change everything around them will also change.

How can a country have a government unable to control its national natural resources and still call it 'a government'? It is reported that,

> "46. The great lakes in DRC have been under heavy fishing pressure for the last three decades. In Lake Edward, for example, at least 30,000 households rely on fishing. About 83 per cent of close to 4,000 fishing boats are illegal." (UNEP-MONUSCO-OSESG, 2015, p.).

What do then the government officials do in the offices? Dozing? Counting money gained from corruption? What do the ministers, vice-ministers, and the members of their cabinet do in the offices? Writing projects that will be funded by western donors? Planning to skill the funded money to buy good houses in western countries? What do the government officials in charge do in their offices if about 83 percent of the fishing boats can be operating illegally in one of their lakes? Where do they think the money to pay the teachers will come from the government cannot effectively control all the natural resources and other economic activities of the country by to make them pay taxes that enrich the public treasure?

That is just the virus of natural resource mismanagement mentality (NRMM) combined with extravagant egoism. We need to be aware of what political leaders with NRMM do when they are elected or appointed to lead the people. They don't build the nation; they just build their belly to be able to give the termites enough fat and healthy meats when their bodies get deteriorated in the coffins after being buried! Even the money they receive from donations to serve general interests of the nation is sent back to the countries of donors for safe-keeping after they have stolen it from the national treasure.

By examining the following quote, we may conclude that the AGLR really need leaders free from the NRMM and able to lead effectively the countries.

> "47. The total fish catch on Lake Edward in 2014 is estimated at about 19,400 tons, at a value of USD 35 million, with an average price of USD 1.8 per kilogram. About 30 percent of this catch is commercialized and the rest consumed locally. If one percent of the commercialized illegal fishery income goes to armed groups and 10 – 30 percent reaches organized crime networks through illegal taxation of transportation or actual fish catch, this amounts to USD 105,000 to militias and about USD one to three million to criminal networks. If roughly the same applies to Lake Albert, Lake Kivu, and Lake Tanganyika the income for armed groups is about USD 420,000, and for criminal networks USD four to twelve million per year from fisheries. Clearly this is an area where there exists a significant information gap, requiring concerted information collection and analysis." (UNEP-MONUSCO-OSESG, 2015, p.).

That is the situation in DRC, a country that mostly depends on foreign aid to run the government and other state institutions while it is losing its citizens and natural resources by the illicit natural resources exploitation! Also, the plundered resources are mostly benefited the foreign plunders than the national ones. "Around 98 percent of the net profits from illegal natural resource exploitation – particularly gold, charcoal and timer – goes to transnational organized criminal networks operating in and outside DRC." (UNEP-MONUSCO-OSESG, 2015, p.4). This situation if not so different from that of the time of Leopold II in the Congo; he used some Congolese in his activities of plundering the natural resources of the country.

The used people were obliged to work hard but the one who took profit for their work was, in fact, Leopold II and his Belgian agents. And the loser was the DRC as a nation; that is why we should be ready to say no to the actual system in the AGLR if we want durable peace and prosperity for all. Leopold II's exploitative philosophy is still in use in order to hinder DRC's progress, and the neighbors should help the country to be free from NRMM because it prospers they also prosper!

To show evidence of the persistence of Leopold II mentality in the AGLR, we can consider some report that puts,

> "Armed groups retain only around two percent – equivalent to USD 13.4 million per annum – of the net profits from illegal smuggling. This income represents the basic subsistence cost for all least 8,000 armed fighters per year, and enables defeated or disarmed groups to continuously resurface and destabilize the region." (UNEP-MONUSCO-OSESG, 2015, p.4).

And do the 99 percent go? Is it not to several Leopold IIs who make the transnational chain of criminal plunders?

I have come to bring you money. I know you need money and guns to continue your business. And you know that I need minerals – especially COLTAN – to continue my business. So, I offer you today 1,500,000 US Dollars as you can see it on this table. Some guns are also available for you. Please, serve me all the minerals that you have gathered up to now!
Oh! No problem. We are ready for such trade. I am the commander in Chief of the movement; I can decide and no one will change my decision. And right now, we are running short of guns. Bring them to us. We have a container full of minerals; you will be satisfied. But please boss, don't change your mind in the future. We need this partnership to continue for it is a win-win situation. It's okay for us!

The DRC does not have serious excuses for not being able to have enough funds to boost their national economy while millions of USD circulating illicitly in the armed group businesses. There are no acceptable reasons for the DRC to rank second last in the Human Development Index. Does it not make shame for the Congolese people especially the political leaders to hear what the world is reporting about their country? For example, when we read that,

> "The country ranks second to last on the Human Development Index (186 out of 187 countries), and its per capita income, which stood at $220 in 2012, is among the lowest in the world. The United Nations estimates that there are some 2.3 million displaced persons and refugees in the country and 323,000 DRC nationals living in refugee camps outside the country. A humanitarian emergency persists in the more unstable parts of the DRC and sexual violence rates remain high." (World Bank – 2015 – DRC Country Overview)

It is known that there is increasing need of cooking energy in the AGRL and people primarily rely on the use of charcoal. And to have charcoals a tree or trees must lose their lives. In the AGLR, DRC with huge forest reserve is the most victim (but not the only) of deforestation due to the needs of energy of the neighboring countries. Most of those countries have no or few natural forests because of their incapacity to preserve them.

So, some people of the countries of AGLR illicitly go to the DRC to supplement their shortage especially in the regions controlled by rebel groups. That is common in the DRC because the leading political leaders seem to be pursuing the same aims with the rebel leaders: their egoistic interests. They all seem to have the natural resource mismanagement mentality. About the charcoals need in the AGLR, the UN Experts report of April 2015 inscribes,

> "48. Charcoal constitutes the primary energy supply for 70-90 percent of households in the Central African region. With rapid population growth and urbanization, the demand for charcoal continues to grow, and is likely to increase threefold by 2050. In neighboring Uganda, Rwanda and Burundi, deforestation is well advanced with most of the natural forests having been cleared. Currently, charcoal consumption in these countries is substantially higher than domestic production and supply." (UNEP-MONUSCO-OSESG, 2015, p.13).

So, should members of the rebel movements be ready to welcome people from neighboring country to help them destroy natural forests of DRC? Should the involved people of Burundi, Rwanda, and Uganda think that going illicitly to DRC for charcoal procurement is the best solution to their needs of energy? Do their leaders think the same? Do they want to participate in the clearing of the natural forests of DRC that contribute too much to the ecosystem of the whole AGLR? Do the AGLR lack enough water in its rivers that can supply electricity to satisfy the regional demand for the domestic need of energy instead of using force or guns to clear natural forests in the DRC?

It is good to remember that all the ancestors of the people of AGLR reached there by migration (except the pygmy people about whom the history is not clear where they migrated from). The ancestors of the people of the AGLR met a good natural environment that did not refuse them the right to live there. They enjoyed living in that region of African as being one of the best places with good natural air in the world... But it is sad to see that their descents are paying back evil to the forests which are always ready to do good for all. They seem to be ignorant of the fact that if the forests die, the people also die! Can we pretend to live in durable peace and prosperity for all with such mentality? Let's examine the following table to find out how people with natural resource mismanagement mentality in the AGLR pose acts of dangerous consequences when they are unable to wisely use the natural resources available to meet their needs, especially the rebel and political leaders.

The examination of the following table about charcoal production in the AGLR shows that the loss of forest of one country concerns indirectly the other because of its impact on regional or international ecosystem, the highest loss of forest is in the DRC. For example, the DRC has recorded 2012 a loss of forest almost ten times higher than that of Uganda while it would be two times higher as its population is almost the double of the Ugandan population in the table.

Official statistics of charcoal production and value compared with forest loss in countries in central African region

Country	Population	Production charcoal metric tons 2012 (FAO)	Ha forest loss 2012 (GFW)	Ha forest loss/Million capita 2012	Ha forest loss per 1000 ton official production of charcoal	Charcoal worth estimate in USD (USD 200-600/ton)
Rwanda	12 000 000	48 000	844	70	18	10 – 29m
DRC	77 400 000	2 167 561	455 058	5 879	210	434– 1,300m
Uganda	36 800 000	600 000	19 202	522	32	120- 360m
Burundi	10 400 000	60 000	755	73	13	12 – 36m

Source: UNEP-MONUSCO-OSESG, 2015, p.14

What is the DRC the most affected by the deforestation than other countries of the AGLR? The answer to this question is found in the UN Experts report of April 2015. It clearly informs that "Over twelve interviews with rangers in Tanzania, Uganda, Rwanda and Burundi confirmed substantial illicit trade, and mainly from DRC going east to Rwanda, Burundi, and Uganda. Only minor traffic of charcoal from Tanzania was reported to these three countries." (UNEP-MONUSCO-OSESG, 2015 p. 14).

People from Uganda, Rwanda, and Burundi illicitly transport charcoal from DRC to their countries. Why? The demand for cooking energy is very high in those countries, and they do not have enough energy supply to meet the national needs of their people. Why? While different people may give different possible reasons, but our humble point of view is that since the independence of these countries of the AGLR, most of their political leaders seem to have difficulties to manage well the natural resources of their countries. Is that Natural Resource Mismanagement Mentality? Yes, because the region has very rich natural resources but the lives of millions of people are more and more worsening, and the countries depend so much on foreign aids! Can you imagine having rare natural resources that some western companies need and without which they cannot have products, but you fail to use that privilege to improve people lives in your countries?

If there are some companies in the West that cannot work without the minerals of the AGLR, then this African region has no reason to experience financial insecurity. The reality should be almost the same with other natural resources like charcoal. No illicil trade should be allowed. Why do some people of the AGLR are very ready to illicitly facilitate the supply of charcoal to foreign countries? To whom does that benefit at the national level of the country?

The UN Experts report of April 2015 engraves "Investigations by UNEP-INTERPOL have estimated threat finance to non-state armed groups from taxing the charcoal trade in the Trans-Sahara is in the range of 111-289 million USD annually. The official transport across border (i.e. import and export) – is in the range, however, of a half to eight truckloads for these countries (UNEP-MONUSCO-OSESG, 2015 p. 14). From this, we learn that the armed rebel groups administrate fiscally the regions that they occupy.

That generate founds to them. Shall we say that it is like having many governments in one state or country? And when that happens no one will seem to be willing to protect what exists for the general interest of all the people of the country. There will always be a tendency of over-exploitation which is very dangerous to everyone in the DRC because of its negative consequences on the environmental components of the country.

However, one of the consequences of the acts of people with NRMM is the destruction of the environmental state of DRC with the serious deforestation that is taking place in the country. What the neighbors in the illicit business of natural resources of the DRC seem to ignore is that 'the Congolese will not be the only losers or victims the deforestation of their country'; people need to know that the oxygen and the good climatic conditions that are generated by the forests of DRC benefit the whole Africa, even the whole world. With few hundreds of dollars in the pockets, plunders may try to think that they have become happy and safe!

That is why all the people and the military groups in the DRC that continue to mismanage the natural resources have to stop; they need to change their mentality and think well about what they are doing because all the natural things that we get from a good management of natural resources are far of great value than money. For example, you cannot pay money to have abundant rain that we all need in the AGRL; but by preserving the existing forests and planting more trees, you can make sure the abundant rain continue to be on your sides.

What are you doing exactly that cannot be immediately stopped? Do you want to kill the whole world including yourself? We need to be ready for positive change because the information concerning the 'massacre of forests' in the AGLR is clear. What you are doing is already revealed. The UN Exports report of 2015 puts,

"53. Several militant groups have in the past relied on taxing of charcoal for income generation, including FDLR, various Mai Mai groups and until recently, ADF also outside their main operating areas. FDLR makes about USD 600,000 per year on taxation of charcoal alone in the Karenga village are, northeast of Goma. The majority of this charcoal was sold in Goma. The National Congress for the Defense of the People, now dissolved, make at least 700,000 USD in one year by controlling the Bunagana border control post to Uganda. They made an estimated USD four million annually on charcoal taxation. There is significant deforestation along the FDLR controlled area along highway N2 Beni-Butembo-Goma, and along N2 Mukoloka-Bukavu. Parts of N3 Bukavu-Kisangani are vital income sectors for FDLR. Mai Mai and FDLR presence is strategically located to enable taxation of charcoal traffic bottlenecks, as well as minerals along road corridors." (UNEP-MONUSCO-OSESG, 2015 p. 14).

Trees in the forests make sure human beings are living better lives. But some human beings in the working hard and sometimes using guns to make sure trees are dying even without replacing them with some new 'baby tries'? What ingratitude and ignorance? So, can you kill them to have money and then claim that you are fighting to defend people? No, you are just fighting to kill both trees and peoples including yourselves! If you could see a little bit further than where you are seeing and think a little bit more deeply and positively about your nations, you would surely have rejected the destructive proposals of the people in the transnational chains of plunders because you are just working for them to destroy your own nations and finally yourselves. Wake up and stand up for positive change. Wake up and stand up to welcome noble principles for durable peace and prosperity for all in your countries. Wake up and stand up to build Africa as true

Africans. Stand up to fight against the plunder of African timbers; everybody is to be concern about that.

Mostly the African political leaders who are also mobilized by Africa Progress Panel in this passage "The 2014 Africa Progress Panel report, *Grain, Fish, Money: Financing Africa's green and bleu revolutions*, calls on Africa's political leaders to take concrete measures now to reduce inequality by investing in agriculture. It also demands international action to end what is describes as the plunder of Africa's timber and fisheries." (Africa Progress Panel – Press Release, nd).

DR Congo is a amazing country. You can enter the forest to cut big trees and no one bother you! It seems in this country, the government is absent. The political leaders are asleep. You see, we are foreigners but we can have woods freely from their forests!
My friend, the trees belong to God. He is the Owner of everything. Let's take advantage of what God created for the people of Congo as they are unable to manage them.

In fact, in the previous paragraphs, we give more details about the natural resources of the DRC and how they have been misused to nurture conflicts in the AGLR. But DRC is not the only country of the AGLR that has been blessed with rich natural resources that are mismanaged.

For example, Uganda has also rich natural resources but the country has been facing serious socioeconomic problems that seem to have made the country to rely on what will come from foreign countries to deal with national challenges. But when we look at what the country has, that was not supposed to be the case if there were a good management of the national resources. It is reported that,

> "Uganda's natural resource base is one of the richest and most diverse in Africa, resulting in the country's economy relying heavily on goods and services so provided. As part of efforts to ensure effective management of Uganda's environment and natural resources, several policies and

institutions have been put in place. Despite these efforts the country's natural resources continue to be degraded, and this jeopardizes both individual livelihoods and the country's economic development." (UNEP, 2010).

We can assume that the people of Uganda, particularly, the political leaders are aware of their total economic dependence on natural resources which are considered to be among the richest and most diverse in Africa. But why then those rich natural resources are not managed to set the country on the path of prosperity for all by improving individual livelihood of the populations especially the most vulnerable ones? What is the problem with these countries of AGLR that they fail to welcome durable peace and prosperity for all while having abundant natural resources? We can humble say for Uganda, as we have just said for the DRC, that the problem of this country is all about people's mentality.

That is why with huge and diverse natural resources, some of the unsatisfied leaders of Uganda continue to smuggle the borders of DRC to take part in the plunder of natural resources of that country. That is why Uganda is failing to provide adequate medical care to its many of its citizens.

It is reported that Uganda ranks among the top 10 countries in the world for high maternal, newborn and child mortality rates. HIV and Aids is now the second leading cause of death among adolescents, accounting for 300 deaths a day (UNAIDS, 2014). Why all these and yet you are rich according to your natural resources? We need to find out whether there is a curse on the countries of AGLR because they seem to share the same fate? Ugandans to have a clear understanding of their problems by finding out why millions of them are not enjoying the richness of their natural resources to live well.

As Africans, we need to understand the fact that we have the leadership responsibility of working hard and hand in hand to make sure everything that we do is done to serve primordially the people regardless their races, tribes, religious beliefs, opinions, etc. And we cannot achieve that with the natural resource mismanagement mentality which often makes most Africans lose while they were supposed to win. That is what continues to revolt our mind when we read that,

> "Uganda loses $899 million worth of productivity per year due to high levels of stunting, iodine-deficiency disorders, iron deficiency, and low birth weight. The percentage of children deprived of access to safe water decreased from 39% to 30% between 2010 and 2013 (MOGLSD et al.), 2014). An emerging concern centers around children with disabilities, whose condition is often the result of ante- and neonatal complications related to capacity constraints in the delivery of basic health services." (MGLSD - Ministry of Gender, Labour and Social Development & UNICEF Uganda, 2015, p. 3)."

There is urgent need of change of mentality for Ugandans as it is for all the people of AGLR. If people with NRMM do not change positively their mentality, they will always be ready to threaten the lives of others; they will always be ready to recruit innocent civilians and make them lose their lives in the pursuit of illicit and egoistic gains from foreign countries.

It is time to refuse to complicate your own lives and those of other people. It is time to say no to negative mindsets and ideologies. It is time to stand for regional stability. It is time to give the best motivation to our children to learn to serve the interests of the country and those of the whole AGLR. It is time to make efforts to educate people who have good mentality which is ready to learn to serve others. All Ugandan adults need to teach good moral lessons to themselves and to the children. That is important because moral virtues should precede any leadership responsibility; and when that is done, the country will be blessed with virtuous and responsible leaders who are well educated and not willing to disturb the peace of others.

The AGLR need brains which are free from conflicts and negative mentalities. Otherwise, the nation will always have huge numbers of children unwilling to learn regardless the efforts of the government to their early education free of charge. A report of MGLSD and UNICEF Uganda analyzing the situation of children in Uganda puts,

> "While Uganda has made important strides in extending primary schooling since universal primary education was introduced in 1997, dropout rates remain high. Early childhood development policies have improved at national level, with implementation and coordination being the next core challenges. Conflict and disasters (natural and man made) continue to undermine and disrupt the provision of

education, as well as the development and well-being of children more generally. Violence in schools is widespread, contributing to high dropout rates and poor performance." (MGLSD & UNICEF Uganda, 2015, p. 6).

We really need positive change of mentality in the AGLR, if not durable peace and prosperity for all will remain an impossible dream. The immediate positive change of mentality is needed concerning the management of natural resources of every country of AGLR because that seems to be the main reason why people fight each other. Is it because some industrialized countries cannot proceed well without using some of what is naturally available in the AGRL and never found elsewhere?

No, if the people with NRMM change positively their minds in the AGLR, those who cannot break through without the raw materials that African region will continue to get what they need, but without the use of guns or any form of violence and theft that impend any initiative for durable peace and prosperity for all. That will help Uganda preserve its natural resources. The World Bank reported that,

> "Ugandans must adopt a mindset of preserving the country's natural resources to move from poverty to prosperity, beginning with potential leaders who must show evidence of having planted trees. This was one of the key resolutions at the end of a recent one-day workshop sponsored by the World Bank Group in partnership with the country's Parliament for Disaster Risk Reduction. The workshop provided 44 Members of Parliament with knowledge and experience in disaster preparedness and management." (Worldbank, 2013, Transforming Poverty to Prosperity by Preserving Uganda's National Resources).

This reality applies to all the countries of AGLR. We have shown in the previous paragraphs of this chapter that there is a serious shortage of cooking energy in Rwanda, Burundi, and Uganda. So, some people from these countries smuggle the borders of the DRC or go to bordering regions controlled by militias to illicitly import charcoal from that country which is still having an important part of its natural forests while Rwanda, Burundi, and Uganda have almost lost theirs. But is that the wise solutions to their need of cooking energy? Do they want DRC to completely lose its natural forests as they have already lost theirs?

Why then the people of the AGLR countries are not planting too many trees while they are aware of the important loss of forests they are victims of? Do they think to live well without abundant trees in their countries? What the World Bank urged Uganda is relevant. We also say the same – please Ugandans plant as many trees as possible – because the forests of DRC cannot suffice for both cooking energy and good oxidation for all the people of AGLR for many years.

We urge all the leaders of Uganda and its neighboring countries to be busy planting trees; otherwise, you are asking to our rich and diverse biodiversity to progressively deteriorate and to kill us all one day. We do not want the natural disasters that happen in the past to take place again. But nothing can stop them from happening again with some people are still living with natural resource mismanagement mentality. It is documented that,

> "In the past two decades more than 200,000 Ugandans were affected by disasters on average each year. According to the Uganda Bureau of Statistics, 65.7% of households experienced at least one type of disaster between 2000 and 2005. In 1987, the drought affected 600,000 people. In 1997, floods affected 153,500 people, killing 100. More recently, the 2008 drought affected 750,000 Ugandans and two years later, landslides in Western Uganda killed over 250 people and affected 350,000 others." (Worldbank, 2013, Transforming Poverty to Prosperity by Preserving Uganda's National Resources).

In addition, we humbly suggest that what is advised to Uganda apply to the whole AGLR. For example, in

Burundi there are also many challenging issues related to natural resource management. "In rural areas, 61.5% of the population cannot meet their basic needs in terms of calorie intake, versus 41% in Bujumbura." (World Bank, 2015, Burundi Country Overview). Why that situation? It is just one of the consequences of the existence of natural resource mismanagement mentality. Burundians need to understand that no one will bring their country to durable peace and prosperity for all if the people with NRMM do not change positively.

It is also the same for Rwanda. About this country, the World Bank reported that "While Rwanda has been effectively using aid for development, the country remains vulnerable to fluctuations in aid flows." (World Bank, 2015, Rwanda Country Overview). The Rwandan Ministry of Natural Resources (2012), in a document entitled '*Land*

Administration System Manual 1. Land Administration Procedures', puts,

> "Being a densely populated and hilly country, Rwanda faces serious problems related to the scarcity of land, the mode of human settlement and the protection of the environment. The evolution of agriculture, long considered as the backbone of the national economy, has become unpredictable because the land resource has been badly managed, and yet over 90% of the Rwandan population work on land from which they earn their livelihood. Soil erosion has worsened due to   continuous cultivation of land, settlement on marginal land that is unsuitable for   agriculture, and lack of reliable soil conservation methods" (page 1).

Conversely, Challender at al. (2003, p.4 – 5) give some recommendation in their report that may be summarized in the following point. To solve the problem of natural resource mismanagement, civil societies, resource-rich governments, donors, international financial institutions, and extractive companies should all be involved in the subsequent activities: there should be,

– institution of full transparency and improved management of mineral resource revenues by governments,

– publication of all payments made by extractive companies and received by governments,

– improving the development impact of business operations (e.g. extractive companies can adhere to international codes/standards concerning corruption, security and human rights, and can work to benefit local businesses and communities in areas of investment),

– ceasing foreign state involvement in the illegal exploitation or mismanagement of mineral resources inside the territory of other states,

– strengthening the capacity of civil society for monitor transparency and improve resource management. But for any good suggestion to work well in the AGLR, people should decide to change.

And decisions should be effectively followed by actions for change of minds requires personal conviction and commitment. So, we all have the responsibility to vulgarize the principles for positive change of mentality if we really believe in durable peace and prosperity for all.

7.2.7. Chronic Laziness and Easy Life Mentality (CLELM)

What is Chronic Laziness and Easy Life Mentality (CLELM) in the AGLR?

The chronic laziness and easy life mentality (CLELM) in the African Great Lakes Region (AGLR) can be defined as a negative state of mind that impends or stops some people from using their physical, intellectual, and spiritual capacity and energy in order to produce goods or services that can help them to be self-reliant and enjoy a good social status. They seem to refuse to feel pain in order to gain. The people with CLELM appear not to be in harmony with themselves and their environments. They dream easy life – a life without sacrifices, without work or pain, without problems to solve – that they are not willing to work for. The next quote mentions the lack of harmony of some Africans that can be also similar to the state of mind of people with CLELM in the AGRL.

> "It could be analogized that just like they shipped away millions of slaves from Africa in exchange of mirrors and tobacco; so, they suck the African blood in exchange for synthetic blood-builders. Consequently, the African person is not in touch both with himself and with his environment. His personality is truncated; his harmony with his environment fragmented." (Okpalike, 2014, p. 81).

The people with CLELM also have dreams of easy life (a prosperous life) that they think can achieve without work and pain. They spend much time reading books, listing to the radios, and watching movies or television channels to learn about Western life that they dream to live without any good initiative or project of development that can result in improving their own African ways of living. They seem to be imitators of the 'western development' without necessary skills, knowledge, motivate, and courage to achieve it.

> "The average African look across the shores of the continent for the kind of life he reads in books and watches in movies in the conviction that his environment is totally impotent and incapacitated to so evolve. His interaction with the West teaches him to stand beside himself in the pursuit of the so-called development." (Okpalike, 2014, p. 81).

So, the people with CLELM live in Africa but their hope for durable peace and prosperity is located in Western countries. That is why they are potential threat to any initiatives that aim to improve the lives of people in Africa. Any African living in the AGLR who need to welcome durable peace and prosperity for all in the region need to make a self-assessment of his or her mind check with he or she is not chained by the chronic laziness and easy life mentality because urgent positive change of mentality is needed.

Characteristics of People with Chronic Laziness and Easy Life Mentality in the AGRL

The Chronic Laziness and Easy Life Mentality in the AGRL manifest itself in the people by the means of exhibition of some or all of the following syndromes (but not limited to that).

- Dreaming easy life (a prosperous life) but not willing to work to achieve it.

- Expecting someone else to work for you or to help you while you are able to do it yourself.

- Counting too much on 'African Socialism' or Ubuntu (it renders null and void).

- Being unwilling to produce because of the availability of what is already produced by others (a tendency to beg to survive while one is healthy to work to be self-reliant).

- Thinking so high of oneself – especially for some educated people thinking higher of themselves by neglecting some jobs that can generate money for themselves to live well –

- Too much talking with an apparent carelessness.

- Need of appearing smarter (very clean with good quality of cloths).

Consequences of Chronic Laziness and Easy Life Mentality (CLELM) in the AGRL

It is evident that Chronic Laziness and Easy Life Mentality in the AGLR is a peace and prosperity destroying state of minds due to some of its characteristics as mentioned in the previous point. That is why it should be part of the vices that need to be eradicated or considerably reduced so that the AGLR may recover from its deadly diseases. The Chronic Laziness and Easy Life Mentality (CLELM) in the AGLR has terrible consequences on the lives of millions of people. They manifest in different ways in public, but mainly with chronic poverty, over population of urban areas by rural exodus, and frequent robbery that sometimes uses fire-guns.

- **Chronic Poverty**

Because of the reluctance to work caused by the CLELM, people with that mentality suffer chronic poverty. They are not like their ancestors who were spending almost the whole day using hoes and panga-knives to get what they need to live. They think they are living a modern life that protects them from feeling pain (due to work) to gain a good living; they seem to forget that they are living in a modern world but have not yet made considerable efforts to live a modern life!

And the world calls their countries 'underdeveloped ones.' We need to know that laziness can be a natural state for some people but the history of human beings on the planet earth shows that lazy people could not survive. The history of the Ancestors of Africans shows that they were hard workers. We also need to frankly and honestly mention that African people of the AGRL are not living in a modern society that can easily provide them with food and shelter; we wonder then how can people who are still struggling to meet their basic needs be dreamers of easy lives with the chains of laziness on their legs and arms! Even those who live in modern societies make stride to fight against laziness to enjoy good social statuses.

- **Overpopulation of urban areas in the AGLR (Rural Exodus)**

People with CLELM who live in the villages and other rural settings of the AGLR do leave their homes to go to seek easy and better life in urban areas where, they think, life is possibly good without work or pain. This phenomenon has created, in the AGLR, many jobless young men in urban areas who are most of time busy robbing, stilling, or involved in illicit activities in order to earn a living.

- **Robbery and theft (sometimes using guns)**

Mostly in urban areas, there are many people with CLELM who live by robbery because they are very lazy to do some pieces of work that can sustain their lives. They sometimes use fire guns to still or rob. They constitute a permanent threat to the security of people and their goods in the AGLR.

7.2.8. Time Mismanagement Mentality (TMM)

"Time is your most valuable personal resource. Use it
wisely because it cannot be replaced."
(Author Unknown)

What is Time Mismanagement Mentality (TMM)?

Have ever wondered about the situation of many people in
the countries of African Great Lakes Region (AGLR) who
seem to fail to achieve their career goals or other useful
goals while they appear to be smart, healthy, and fit for
work? Have ever discovered that, in the AGLR, the people
who work to only meet their basic needs (e.g. food,
clothes, shelter, medicine, water, etc.) seem to be more
numerous than those who work to achieve some goals in
their lives? Can we assume that some human beings exist
on the planet earth just to consume the oxygen, food,
water, etc. and then die after working for that while others

work to successfully meet their basic needs and at the same time fulfill some industrious personal life goals that benefit all the community?

It sounds less important to be reminded that human activities are only possible when there is life. And life is the most precious thing that people have; it is valuable than any other thing we can think about and exist in time. To the question 'What is time?', Adair and Allen (2004, p.5) give the following remark, "Time is our lives as measured out in years, months, days, hours, minutes and seconds. What could be more important to you than using this free gift of time effectively, generously and wisely?" Time is among the unchangeable and untouchable things that exist; it is very powerful human capacity because all human beings are fated to submit to its course.

It can be presumed all human beings are enslaved by time because they cannot exist out of it! But regardless the enslaving power of time over human beings, they still have the ability and freedom to exist in it smartly by doing some pleasing and productive activities with wise allocation of a certain amount of time to each of them using other resources that are available in the environment to achieve some personal or community set goals; that is what can be called 'time management'.

In this section, what is called 'Time Mismanagement Mentality' (TMM) refers to the state of mind of some people of the African Great Lakes Region (AGLR) that paralyze any efforts to make goals or/and plans and stick on them with the personal decision or courage of seeing their successful accomplishment on the time already set. The TMM doesn't mean lack of time management skills or lack of skills for setting goals or making plans; it's nor the lack of natural abilities to think well or to speak well neither the result of social discrimination or enslavement. It makes people to naively believe that things will make themselves happen someday!

And people with time mismanagement mentality (TMM) seem to believe that by being so patient, life will be better one day in the future! And some religions help the people with TMM in their weak and negative state of mind by providing more teachings that postpone God's blessings and make them more hopeful for a future they are not working for and without no goals and plans at all! That attitude impedes the establishment of durable peace and prosperity for all, and we need to address it very sincerely to help the African people to discover that they are the solutions to their problems. There is no time to waste waiting for international solutions to our local and national problems; we need to completely change our mentalities on how we use the time that God has given us.

Anthony (2015, p. 131) writes "If Africa must be like other civilizations that have taken advantage of temporal conditions to build artifacts that have stood the test of time and the vicissitudes of human history, she must change her mentality towards time. Africa's development is tied to her management of time." That is very important to consider when thinking about any possible peace and prosperity initiative in Africa. We have to be honest when addressing serious issues like time mismanagement mentality. Instead of being busy blaming the colonialists and the post-colonial leaders for their destructive acts that can be considered as the origin of African problems, it is wiser for Africans to look first at themselves; they need to get rid of all that do not help them to adequately fight against hunger, ignorance, and disease in the continent. Anthony (2015, p. 259) puts,

> "This notwithstanding, as Africans discuss how Europe underdeveloped Africa, it could also be a worthwhile discussion to focus on how Africans underdeveloped and are under-developing Africa. Major issues to be considered could be how Africans are under-developing Africa through corruption, ill-focused leadership, war, religious crisis etc. While these are fundamental factors in the issue of Africa's development, this piece focuses on the issue of time-consciousness. Nyasami (2010) wrote that "No meaningful progress can be achieved in the absence of a well-coordinated program that is managed within the specifications of time and space".

Likewise, good management of time is needed in the African Great Lakes Region (AGLR). All the populations of the AGLR should be good managers of time; they are to be good time planners in order to be efficiently productive. Schermerhorn (2007, p.4) defines 'a manager' as a person who supports and is responsible for the work of others.

From this definition, we can suggest that a 'time manager' in the AGLR is supposed to be only responsible of his or her time by supporting it by good goals and plans with good time management skills. That is so important for nations that need to reach durable peace and prosperity for all in the AGLR.

It is very necessary for all Africans to become good time-keepers for the African continent have been losing too much time working to for the interested of colonialists, explorers, and some missionaries since its discovery by Europeans; so, in Africa there is a crucial need of recovering from socioeconomic illnesses that this continent have been suffering since long ago. The eradication of time mismanagement mentality (TMM) is one of the most powerful and effective curative treatment that should be used to heal the African continent.

As other negative mental attitudes in Africa, the TMM requires personal decision and effort after being aware of its consequences that hinder personal, community, and national progress. Every African of the AGLR who fills concerned with TMM and with the willingness to help in the process of establishment of durable peace and prosperity in the region will contribute to that by taking decision for himself or herself first and helping others to change by showing them the consequences of stubbornness.

In fact, we do not need to create reasons to justify why we continue to keep what is not helping us to prosper. There is nothing that can be considered to be noble or of great cultural value if it is impeding the development of our communities, our countries. Even the habits or things that we consider very meaningful for us because they are from parents, grandparents, or ancestry, etc. need to be destroyed forever if they are cannot allow us to live in peace and prosperity; they are as destructive as demons. That is why change is really needed; it could be very productive for the people of the African Great Lakes Region to understand that Africa is in urgent need to positive change of mentality.

Time mismanagement mentality will always keep many Africans far behind — in terrible lack — if they do not make vigorous strides towards good time management. Anthony (2015, p. 131) inscribes "The direct consequence of this attitude towards time is Africa's underdevelopment. If Africa must be like other civilizations that have taken advantage of temporal conditions to build artifacts that have stood the test of time and the vicissitudes of human history, she must change her mentality towards time. Africa's development is tied to her management of time."

People can agree or disagree with Anthony, but the truth about Africa is known and some good African observers can be able to recognize that millions of Africans are still letting time passes without making good use of it. "You can't enjoy the benefits of time management if you allow your valuable time to slip away." (Schermerhorn, 2007, p.97).

Anthony writes about Mbiti's definition of potential time and actual time and his viewpoint concerning African time showing that Africans are more interested and preoccupied with the past things or events rather than the future ones. He puts,

> "According to Mbiti, potential time is that which has the likelihood of immediate occurrence or

which lies within the category of natural phenomenon. The actual time is what is present and what is past, revealing the African time as that which moves backward rather than forward. This would mean that Africans set their minds on things that have passed rather than on the future. Thus the African understands time as consisting of a long past and a present with virtually no future. This contrasts with the Western concept of time which is linear, consisting of an indefinite past, the present and infinite future. For the African, the future is absent since it has not been realized." (Anthony, 2015, p. 129).

This being the case for African time, it can be said that without change of mentality concerning time Africans with time mismanagement mentality will never be able to make good and successful plans to achieve their visions and goals. People who consider future to be absent because it has not been realized are not so different from those who let things happen rather than making them happen! Those kinds of people in the AGLR need to change otherwise they will always be poor and their contribution to durable peace and prosperity for all in the region will be none. Those are some of the people who constitute a burden to the states while having rich potentials that could be exploited to enrich themselves and their countries.

It is a pity for many African nations because even the people who are supposed to be good 'role model' in terms of time management are reported to be 'great time killers'. Anthony (2015, p. 131) writes,

> "In many government owned ministries, many Africans who should be working in their offices during working hours are seen sitting under the tree discussing. It is in this regard that Victor (2013) observed that "African time lingers around like an awful smell that will just not go away. Everywhere you go you see examples of tardiness that can be linked back to the myth of African Time. What is particularly distressing is that the African Time bug has arrived at many schools. As you drive past a school you see a group of children casually walking over well past the official starting time. The tragic thing about those who arrive late is that they are invariably the first to leave school for their homes. Worst still, many senior officials in both politics and business seem to delight in

arriving late, as if this confirmed their status. Politicians habitually fail to be on time for virtually every program — especially given that so many of them whizz past the traffic at the flick of their blue lights and their loud sirens" (p. 5).

Although some Africans are making effort to fight against being late at work, many are still not really carrying about being on time to their professional settings. Why? That is just the result of time mismanagement mentality (TMM). As it is shown by Anthony, in the African Great Lakes Region (AGLR) there are millions of workers who fail to be fruitful as expected by their states because of not respecting time.

Political leaders appear to be among the most time killers in the AGLR although in most of their speeches there are always words like 'development', 'progress', 'decent work', 'good pay', 'good quality health', etc. You may wonder how a person who is suffering from TMM disease can help people to be developed, to progress, to have decent works and good pays, etc. while himself or herself is not living a luxurious life because of good time management and hard work but because of corruption, plunder, etc.

It is really surprising to hear some plunderers and corrupt political leaders preach people to have good use of time to develop the country or putting in their speeches words that support durable peace and prosperity for all with almost no respect for the time that God gave them to build their nations! Is it not a poisonous state for leaders to be very rich without no work, no time management, and no investment at all? What kind of leaders can they be when they do not have respect for their time and that of others? How did they because rich? How can they inspire their followers to make them give useful contributions to the prosperous development of their countries?

If you never learn about the time mismanagement mentality of many political leaders in the AGLR, make a careful observation of how they behave and you will make your own conclusion. These people should change their negative mentality so that the region may be a pool of durable peace and prosperity for all; if not willing to change, those fake political leaders are to be professionally made inactive or removed from the AGLR to stop being barriers…

It is time for change and we do not have more hours to waste. Such leaders political and any other leaders with such mentality must understand that they are the ones who continue to make Africa an underdeveloped continent, and not the non-Africans. And the millions of Africans who continue to be taken in hostage by those fake leaders who make them waste time by an infinite blame of Europe for its historical negative acts and practices in African should free themselves.

All African should understand that we do not need to waste time looking to the past and remain there! We should look to the future because we shall never live in the past to be subdued by it. But the future is waiting for us and we should be able to subdue it for the durable peace and prosperity for all using the gift of dominion that God gave us. We should be able to dominate time by making good goals and plans for the future, not for the past!

We should not be the ones who are destroying Africa and then accuse the people who exploited it for their egoistic interests in the past because the political leadership of the continent is now in the hands of African leaders. Anthony (2015, p. 130 – 131) mentions almost the same by putting,

> "A cursory glance at Mbiti's African idea of time as backward very much explains why Africans are more concerned with how Europe underdeveloped Africa than with how they are themselves destroying the future of Africa through corruption. We are often more concerned with a history that has passed than with a future that is full of opportunities. If the greatest emphasis of the African is on the past rather than the future, and if on the future at all, on the immediate future, it means that the vision that Africans have for themselves cannot but be limited. And obviously, where there is no vision, there is no development."

That is very important to note. African Great Lake Region (AGLR)'s durable peace and prosperity for all cannot be achieved with the mentality of bad management of time. And any good time management requires the existence of visions, goals, and plans; that is what we are going to address in the next points of this chapter with reference to the people with time mismanagement mentality in the AGLR.

Characteristics of People with Time Mismanagement Mentality (TMM) in the African Great Lakes Region (AGLR)

"To value time as your most precious commodity – to be spent both carefully and generously should be an essential element in your philosophy of life."
(Adair & Allan)

Many people suffer the consequences of time mismanagement mentality (TMM) in the African Great Lakes Region (AGLR) without realizing it. Or they think to be living a normal life. Why? Maybe it is because the manifestation of the Time Mismanagement Mentality has a strong link with certain habits or characteristics that they believe are right for their personal and community development. Those characteristics may be explained but not limited to lack or weak purposes, visions, goals, and plans in life; lack or weak personal commitment to purposes, visions, goals, and plans; tendency to do everything oneself; misconception or misunderstanding of providence.

✓ **Lack or Weak Purposes, Visions, Goals, and Plans**

People with time mismanagement mentality (TMM) in the African Great Lakes Region (AGLR) sometimes manifest their state of mind about time by failing to have clear and outstanding life purposes, visions, goals, and plans. Many people in the AGLR live as if they were accidentally on the planet earth and that is one of the main reasons why some of them do not think of time as valuable and rare. That is why they do not use wisely the time that God has given; because they don't know or they know but the neglect the noble assignment that they have to do on earth before leaving it, many destroy their own lives and the lives of others by not aiming to pursue their assignments with plans to achieve their goals. For the people with TMM, durable peace and prosperity is and will remain elusive if no positive change takes place in their minds.

Nonetheless, it is necessary to have a good time management when we have to expect a future of stable peace and prosperity in the AGLR. To do that well, clear and outstanding purposes, visions, goals, and plans should be used with much consideration. There many words that can be used when we think about time management; but the words like purpose, vision, goal, and plan always come to mind of time planners who need success in their lives.

As you can see in the following chart, Adair and Allen (2004) give some ten key-words for time planners; but we are only going to focus on four among them to illustrate the peace and prosperity killing behaviors of people with time mismanagement mentality (TMM) in the African

Great Lakes Region (AGLR).

<table>
<tr><td colspan="1" align="center">Ten key-words for time planners</td></tr>
</table>

Ten key-words for time planners
The English language is not a great help when it comes to thinking clearly in this area. There are a variety of overlapping words, but they have overtones, so choose your words carefully! Here are some of the runners:
1 Purpose Either a resolute, deliberate movement towards a result or the desired result itself. Conveys too, the idea of significance or meaning.
2 Goal A deliberately selected result that can be won only with difficulty by dedicated and prolonged effort. In a vague sense: the general trend a person or group takes.
3 Aim A mark or target to be aimed at, thus an object or purpose. The purpose directing of effort.
4 End The intended effects of actions often in distinction or contrast to means.
5 Object May equal end but often applies to a more individual determined wish and may nearly mean motive.
6 Objective Something tangible, specific and immediately attainable, towards which effort is directed.

7 Mission A task assigned or undertaken. The purpose for which one was sent. (Mission comes from the Latin verb 'to send'.)
8 Plan Sets of ideas developed to accomplish a desired result. The most informal and the most general of a set of such words: blueprint, design, program, proposal, scheme.
9 Vision Unusual discernment or foresight/sharpness of understanding. A mental concept of a distinct or vivid kind; a highly imaginative scheme or anticipation.
10 Intention Little more than what one has in mind to do or bring.

Source: Adapted from Adair and Allen (2004, p. 15 – 16)

- **Purpose, Vision, Goal, and Plan**

Let's look at the dictionary definitions of these words to figure out their basic meanings and how they are connected with time. The online source, www.dictionary.reference.com, defines 'Purpose' as the reason for which something exists or is done, made, used, etc. In this definition, we can observe that all the verbs used (exist, do, make, use) to give explanation of the word 'purpose' have a strong relationship with 'time'. We need time to exist; we need time to do or to make something; and to use the made or created things, we also need time. And all that is done with a purpose! The word 'purpose' is also defined as something set up as an object or end to be attained (Merriam-Webster Dictionary and Theraurus, 2006).

The word 'Vision' is the act or power of sensing with the eyes; sight. It is the act or power of anticipating that which will or may come to be (www.dictionary.reference.com). In this definition, the word 'vision' is connected to the future events, things, opportunities, etc. And all have something to do with time without which they will not exist or happen. Vision is also defined as something seen otherwise than by ordinary sight (as in a dream or trance); it is a vivid picture created by the imagination; it is the act or power of imagination; it is the unusual wisdom in foreseeing what is going to happen (Merriam-Webster, 2006). Goal is defined by www.dictionary.reference.com as the result or achievement toward which effort is directed; aim; end. It is something you hope or plan to achieve. And plan is a scheme or method of acting, doing, proceeding, making, etc. developed in advance. It is a drawing or diagram showing the parts or details of something; it is a method for accomplishing an objective (Marriam-Webster, 2006).

The idea of effort in order to achieve something conveyed by the word 'goal' and that of method of acting or scheme produced by the word 'plan' in the above definitions will have true meaning with time. It can be clearly noticed that time management needs purpose, vision, goal, and plan. So, people with time mismanagement mentality (TMM) in the African Great Lakes Region (AGLR) should be aware of the power that comes from a good time management using proper purposes, visions, goals, and plans to succeed at the right time. Without that the dreams for durable peace and prosperity for all in the AGLR will remain non-achieved.

Moreover, if people are really willing to change, something good will happen. Changing people's attitude about time in AGLR is the work of people themselves. We can work as agents of change by addressing some serious peace and prosperity destroying facts, but the concerned people should decide about their own fates. When we talk about the people with time mismanagement mentality (TMM), we are not mentioning the persons who most of time or sometimes waste time in the AGLR; but we are talking about the people whose beliefs and daily behaviors always show that time is not their most important resources and mostly do let things happen for them rather than making them happen. Even if they are skilled with time management principles, the people with TMM never use them due to their negative mentality or beliefs about time and success in life. Most of them do not have purposes, visions, goals, and plans; some may have them, but with a poor or no understanding of their meanings. And some people with TMM who clearly and correctly understand the importance of having purpose, vision, goal, and plan are seriously committed to their adequate use due to the virus of TMM in their minds; and that has nothing to do with the educational level of people. Why?

Maybe because most of the educated people of the AGLR are confused about what they exist for on this planet earth. I can be said that when we discover why we exist on earth, we become aware of our individual missions that makes the core of our personal purposes in this world; and purposes that we establish with the light from our visions help us to set wise goals that we should reach using effective and efficient plans in order to fulfill our missions on earth.

However, the most important issue here is to discovering our true missions on earth that will allow us to establish purposes. This seems to be very crucial to know by the category of people of the African Great Lakes Region (AGLR) who live without any knowledge of their specific missions in their communities. And all should be reminded that no one is supposed to have a 'mission' with purposes of destroying all the people of different ethnic groups and of plundering the natural resources of the countries of the AGLR!

In addition, all the purposes are supposed to be noble ones – putting the betterment of the lives of human beings and even other physical living creature at the center (for example trees and wild animals) – because God did not create human beings to be destroyers but good leaders and managers with the dominion mandate.

It is known that the majority of the people of the AGLR are Christian as it was shown in the previous chapters of this book. Does their God tell them to live without purpose with alarming waste of time? Or Did He tell them to have destructive purposes, visions, goals, and plans rather than constructive ones? Is He a Supporter of Human Butchers? Even the Muslims and people of other religions in the AGLR will not be able to demonstrate that their God or gods is such category. What is happening in people's minds there if the AGLR should continue to suffer the consequences of time mismanagement mentality while other nations of the world are wisely using their times to produce wonderful things? Are the people of AGLR living in the same world with the good time planners? Don't they have access to the good books of leadership and management? Don't they have access to the sources of information that teach good principles of time management?

There is a problem; we need to agree and to will to change. We need to go through what we know and believe about purposes, visions, goals, and plans and how we use them in our time management habit. How do we establish purposes in life? What are these four words represent for every person of the AGLR? Bob (2003) puts,

> "As you go through life, you don't just pick up things you like doing by chance. You discover what

you're good at because you were *meant* to discover it, just as you were meant to figure out what your fingers do, and how your elbows work. Your unique gifts are hardwired into your system just as surely as your lungs are given their blueprint to breathe. And it's from these specific talents and gifts that you're able to define and determine your definite purpose … the reason why you're here. What's in you cannot be found in another living human being."

Purposes, visions, and goals are established by looking into oneself. We don't need to waste time by going up and down to see what people are doing so that we may also start doing it. That will only be a lamentable waste of time. The gifts and talents we have are very important in the process of eradicating the time mismanagement mentality (TMM).

We need to discover them because they are the directors of our purposes, visions, and goals. By the way, it is good to be aware that there is an important link between purposes, visions, and goals. Bob (nd) explains,

"The vision represents the total journey that you are taking. Goals are the progressive stepping-stones that help you realize your vision, keeping it crystal clear. You could say the vision represents what you are doing with your life, the goal represents the various aspects of how you're doing it and your purpose explains why. It is very important that your purpose, vision, and goals are in harmony."

From the explanation of Bob, we can vision should give a clear picture of what a person is doing or have to do in his or her life; and the purpose should give clear reasons showing why the vision is to be followed; and the goal (s) must let somebody see plainly everything that is to be achieved in order to reach the purpose – that is the fulfillment of one's mission – that gives meaning to the vision.

That is what helps anyone who wisely uses time. The people with time mismanagement mentality (TMM) in Africa can do better if they make up their minds by taking serious decision to change; they will also need to discover the purpose on planet earth (their gifts – work – mission – which will make them more useful to others in their communities), to understand and use the time management skills with apparent purposes, visions, goals, and plans to establish durable peace and prosperity for all.

We need to be earnestly and courageously following our personal visions and work hard to reach our goals because we are supposed to much love for them; they give meaning to our lives. About love for purpose, vision, and goal, we can read,

> "It's absolutely essential that the goal is something you want. There's no playing it safe by simply going after what you THINK you can do. You've got to want it. And you want it because it's moving you in the direction of your vision. It's not just getting a nicer car or earning an extra dollar – your goal is something you dearly want, it's your heart's *desire*. It's helping you *move* in the direction of your vision. Your vision was established with a long-term view of doing the thing you love doing, day in and day out on

purpose, because your purpose is doing what you truly love to do." (Bob Poctor, 2003).

So, if people have true purposes, visions, and goals they don't need outside motivators to archive them. Their inner attitudes serve as the first and great motivation for their success. That is why some leaders in the African Great Lakes Region (AGLR) who are failing to reach the goals set for the development of their countries or communities will have no evident explanation for their lack of motivation which makes some of them waste time or become lazy. Maybe they are not supposed to be where they are. Maybe they are not supposed to be doing the work they have been doing.

The right person at the right place will have the right purpose to fulfill the right goals following his or her right vision to serve the people with love. That kind of person will be free from the time mismanagement mentality because they know well what is most important and have wise ways of deciding what is more valuable for them and the whole community they are serving.

All the same, having the capacity of deciding what is more crucial and more valuable for oneself and the community is an important asset to have. Clarifying what's more important require tact and wisdom. Benfari (2013) writes that the social scientist Milton Rokeach (1979) has devoted his professional life to the study of values and came up with the conclusion there is a difference between human beings in the way they organize their values into hierarchies or priorities. He inscribes that all humans have both end values (beliefs about ultimate goals or desirable states such as happiness or wisdom) and instrumental values (beliefs about what we must do to achieve those end values, such as behaving honestly or responsibly).

The fact that we can obviously agree that humans have differences in clarifying what is valuable for them and their communities may be the proof that the values of organizations or governments may also differ from personal values of peoples. So, when people work in organizations or governments with values that conflict with their personal ones, they are likely to behave like having time mismanagement mentality (TMM). That is why any efficient and effective use of time in organizations or governments requires the conformity of personal values and the values of the institution in which you will be working.

Benfari (2013, p. 228) writes "If you wish to begin clarifying your own values, begin with Rokeach's list and follow these five steps:

2. Step 1. Start with the list of end values and rank-order them from most preferred to least preferred.

3. Step 2. Rank-order the instrumental values the same way. Do not mix values across the list.

4. Step 3. Look over the lists and reorder any values that you think need to be changed.

5. Step 4. Now go through the same ranking process for your organization's end and instrumental values.

6. Step 5. Compare your personal values to the espoused values of your organization."

End values and Instrument Values (Rokeach's list)

End values	Instrument Values
A comfortable life	Ambition
A prosperous life	Hard work and aspiration
Equality	Broad-mindedness
Brotherhood and equal	Open-mindedness;

opportunity	appreciation of diversity
An exciting life A stimulating, active life	Capability Competence; effectiveness
Family security Taking care of loved ones	Cheerfulness Light-heartedness; joy
Freedom Independence and free choice	Cleanliness Neatness and tidiness
Health Physical and mental well-being	Courageousness Standing up for one's beliefs
Inner harmony Freedom from inner conflict	Forgiveness Willingness to pardon others
Mature love Sexual and spiritual intimacy	Helpfulness Working for the welfare of others; Caring and compassion
National security Protection from attack	Honestly Sincerity and truthfulness; trustworthiness
Pleasure An enjoyable, leisurely life	Imagination Creativity and daring
Salvation Saved; eternal life	Intellectualism Self-reliance; self-sufficiency
Self-respect Self-esteem	Logic Consistency; rationality
A sense of accomplishment A lasting contribution	Love Faithfulness to friends or the groups; Respectfulness

Social recognition Respect and admiration	Loyalty Faithfulness to friends
True friendship Close companionship	Obedience Sense of duty
Wisdom A mature understanding of life, Education	Politeness Courteousness; good manners; Respectfulness
A world at peace A world free of war and conflict	Responsibility Dependability and reliability
A world of beauty Beauty of nature and the arts	Self-control Restraint; self-discipline

"Note: The end and instrument values are listed in alphabetical order. There is no one-to-one correspondence between end and instrumental values."
Source: Benfari (2013, p. 230).

Thus, all the people of the African Great Lakes Region in need of peace and prosperity will be ready to change any mentality that is not helping them to adequately use time, if not their dreams to live well by enjoying what God has put in the environment of their countries will never be lived! And to avoid conflicting situations concerning personal values and the values of the institutions, there is a crucial need of making sure the two set of values converge.

Otherwise, there will be the risk of behaving like people with time mismanagement mentality which is durable peace and prosperity killing attitude. About personal values and the values of organizations, Benfari (2013, p. 230) inscribes,

> "Your values and the organization's values should be largely congruent, otherwise you'll experience a feeling of conflict between what you and the organization believe. When such dissonance arises, you have to somehow justify continuing to work there either by denial or by rationalization. Both these defenses lead to an uncomfortable feeling of not doing what is instinctively right for you."

That is very important to know for the people of the AGLR who need to make a positive professional impact in the process of establishing durable peace and prosperity for all in the region. No one has been able to stop the course of time and no one will be; that is why we need to make good use of it for its lost cannot be recovered.

'Plan' as a Time-saving tool and Planning Process

People with time mismanagement mentality (TMM) in the African Great Lakes Region (AGLR) seem to be content or satisfied with the present life situation and forget to plan for a better future with consideration of some useful lessons from the past. That attitude cannot help establish durable peace and prosperity for all in the AGLR. We have experienced dangerous events taking place in the region due carelessness and time-wasting attitude. That attitude which is mostly characterized by a lack of plans or the existing of plans that are not respected by the planners and their followers has resulted in lamentable poverty, disease, and insecurity for many in the AGLR.

A temporarily national tranquil and security does not mean the country will experience the same state all the time in the future. Also, the past unhappy events of a country are not unimportant for the planners to neglect in the process of making plans for durable peace and prosperity for all the citizens. For example, in a political meeting, a political leader who promises that the suppressed rebel groups responsible for past atrocities will never exist again in the country is likely to be considered as a potential liar. Why? Only God can speak with certainty about future events. Humans cannot predict what will happen in the future with exactitude. Only God can do that.

That is why most of the speeches of political leaders of the African Great Lake Region (AGLR) are not durable peace and prosperity conveying tools. We cannot trust them for a future national safety and economic abundance. We need to wisely consider events of the past and to be realistic with the present situation so that we can make good plans that will help us save time, and build a better future for ourselves and the people we are supposed to serve. We do need neither to waste time and get lost in the present nor to rush into the future without a judicious use of our capacities and resources.

Schermerhorn (2007, p. 96) says it this way "It can be easy to get so engrossed in the present that we forget about the future. Yet a mad rush to the future can sometimes go off track without solid reference points in the past." While an English adage teaches that we should let sleeping dogs lay, we are not supposed to look at the past with much interest; we are not supposed to consider past events as more important than future ones. We cannot live in the past but the future is waiting for us to live it. That is why any past dreams or any dreams that convey information concerning what had already happened are less important than the ones that are informing us about the future.

It is known that millions of Africans today continue to waste time talking and blaming the while colonialists for what they did to the African people and the continent, but is that a wise way of progressing into the future? We need to be part of the Africans who believe that it is not over for Africa! We can do better and become competitive in the global market of today's world. Okeneme (2013, p. 161) has mentioned the same situation about many Africans by putting it this way,

> "While many Africans are quick and eager to heap their problems and predicaments on the altar of colonialism, many others yet reject this pessimistic viewpoint and are of the strong opinion that African countries should stop blaming their lack of development on colonialism and seek for positive ways of moving their nations forward."

We should be able to be free from the events of the past by considering them only for reference; we have to be busy for the planned events for the future and consider them for preference. Schermerhorn gives good advice by putting, "We should blend past experiences and lessons with future aspirations and goals, and be willing to adjust as new circumstances arise. He writes that the management process of planning helps us do just that. And it is a process of setting goals and objectives, and determining how to best accomplish them." (Schermerhorn, 2007, p. 96). So, the past is supposed to be referential for the sake of improving the present and the future preference; that is what will help us to move our purposes, visions, and goals at hand with realistic and working plans, which are very important for us by their time saving role, towards a successful future.

Likewise, anyone who needs durable peace and prosperity in the African Great Lake Region (AGLR) can be advised to have a good plan that will help save time and fulfill peace and prosperity purposes, visions, and goals. Schermerhorn (2007) writes that a good planning makes us action-oriented, priority oriented, advantage oriented, and change oriented.

Action-oriented means that we should have a results-driven sense of direction; in other words, every means that will be used should get us to the fulfillment of our goals (results). Priority oriented is about making sure the most important things get our first attention; that being the case, we should be so wise to know what is most important to be done first. With 'Advantage oriented' attitude, we are advised to be ensured that all resources are used to best advantage; by this planning requirement, we should manage well the resources we have by avoiding making less important spending or wastes because misuse of resources have strong link with time mismanagement or loss of time. And by being change-oriented, we shall anticipate problems and opportunities so they can be best dealt with. So, with consideration to what has been mentioned in the previous paragraphs, what is planning in just one sentence?

Schermerhorn (2007, p. 96) inscribes "Said a bit differently, planning involves looking ahead, identifying exactly what you want to accomplish, and deciding how to best go about it." Let's have a look at the steps in the planning process stated in the following table.

STEPS IN THE PLANNING PROCESS	
Step 1. Define your objectives	Know where you want to go; be specific enough to know you have arrived when you get there and how far off you are along the way.
Step 2. Determine current status vis-à-vis objectives	Know where you stand in reaching the objectives; identify strengths that work in your favor and weaknesses that can hold you back.
Step 3. Develop premises regarding future conditions	Generate alternative scenarios for what may happen; identify for each scenario things that may

	help or hinder progress toward your objectives.
Step 4. Make a plan	Choose the action alternative most likely to accomplish your objectives; describe what must be done to implement this course of action.
Step 5. Implement the plan and evaluate results	Take action; measure progress toward objectives as implementation proceeds; take corrective actions and revise plan as needed.

Source: (Schermerhorn, 2007, p. 97)

Every person of the African Great Lakes Region needs to have reasonable life objectives or goals that have to be achieved; each objective or goal that will need people to make good use of time to fulfill should have good reasons. That is very important because of the high value of time. As Okeneme (2013, p. 162) puts "Without reason, man could be said to be an empty being devoid of rationality and may not make rational and positive contributions towards the betterment of his immediate environment."

- **Lack or Weak Personal Commitment to Purposes, Visions, Goals, and Plans**

The lack or weak personal commitment to purposes, visions, goals, and plans are another form of manifestation of the time mismanagement mentality in the African Great Lakes Region (AGLR). This attitude is common for many people with time mismanagement mentality (TMM) in the AGLR. They seem take everything for granted; they take life cheaply and think even if they are not seriously committed to what they have planned according to their purposes, visions, and goals things will still happen.

Ignorantly, they seem to have a negative belief that gods or the province will make them reach their life purposes even if they are making little or no effort!

So, these kinds of people eat too much, sleep too much, drink too much, rest too much, relax too much, and most of time go to any public meeting or gathering even without wise aim. They are always ready to do different things that are not helping them to reach their known life purpose and their assigned life goals. They neglect to respect the plans established for personal success; that is what they regularly do because for most of them, success comes without much effort. Oh, it is a pity for them and for the AGLR because most of them die without reaching their life purposes!

People with lack or weak commitment to their personal life purposes, visions, goals, and plans are a permanent threat to durable peace and prosperity of themselves and others; this can be explained by the fact that they are likely to produce time mismanagement acts that will become distraction or disturbance for other people.

Also, this is sometimes very common for many people in the region, particularly those in leadership positions in public sectors. In the companies that belong to the state in the DRC for example, you don't need to ask when the top and middle line leaders come to work; at what time they are supposed to arrive, and at what time they should leave the workplace. Some of these managers or leaders seem to ignore that their exaggerated absence at work may impede the performance or the progress of institutions they are in charge. They seem to have almost no personal commitment to the purposes, visions, goals, and plans of their organizations. Some of them even behave like 'withdrawers' financial agents' who are just busy asking how much money is there so that they can take some and knock off!

They are well-organized time-waters who do nothing to fight against poverty and ignorance in the AGLR. These people with mostly university degrees do not show good examples of time management, not because they don't have the skills of time management, but because they are enchained in their own minds with time mismanagement mentality (TMM) which will never help their communities or countries to settle in the paths of durable peace and prosperity for all. The top and middle managers of the state's organizations that are supposed to work hard to boost up the economic capacity of their governments do waste time in bars and good places relaxing and enjoying endlessly while projects of public interest and development remain on papers in their offices instead of making serious follow for their execution. And what is the result? The poor citizens are the ones who continue to suffer from famine, diseases, lack of homes, insecurity, poverty.

That same character is sometimes seen in the day to day professional lives of some government officials. From the president to the lowest rank of the political leaders in the governing team of politicians, you sometimes see a serious waste of time which can be considered as a lack of commitment or a weak one. Every now and then, you can wonder whether these people with state responsibilities are really committed to build the country or to make it more and poorer with their lamentable way of working.

Irregular and absent in the offices, and when they present and regular, they mostly deal with financial and immoral issues (corruption, theft of funds, sexual abuses); things or activities that will continue to help them waste the time that could be used to work on purposes, visions, goals, and plans that serve the common interest of the general population. It's a pity if there is no change of mentality for that kind of leadership in the African Great Lakes Region (AGLR). It will continue to be sorry for the region if the people will continue to have 'bad role model' of leadership characterized with a grave waste of time.

We have to address this issue seriously because the country cannot enjoy national peace and prosperity for all with such leaders. For example, a president of a country who is wasting his time to collecting illicitly or illegally money from corruption, theft, and any other means will never help the citizen to prosper. This kind of president, instead of using wisely his time to serve the common interests of the citizens, will always mismanage his time by serving the interests of the foreign investors who bribe him! How? These foreign bosses will never obey the laws of the country; and because they know very well that that president is a thief, they will also be stilling the wealth of the country. And that will be done without fear because they are sure to give more corruption in case they are caught stilling! What kind of political leadership? Total waste of time!

- **Tendency to do Everything Oneself**

Some people in the African Great Lakes Region (AGLR) behave as if they were all-knowing and able to do anything. Whether employed by organizations or self-employed, they have a professional vice that is can be characterized by the two following adjectives: omniscient and omnipotent. That is a clear sign of being infected by time mismanagement mentality virus because no human being can be omniscient or omnipotent. Only God knows everything and is able to do everything he wishes. It is wise to honestly recognize that we are not perfect and capable beings who can do everything. Each person has his or her personal limitations and needs to be aware of his or her weaknesses and strengths.

When doing works, whether for certain companies or for our personal initiatives, we have to be able to identify what we are not able to do or what we cannot do competently so that we may delegate them to people who are able to do them efficiently and effectively. If we don't do that, we shall be wasting time and that will be against our personal development towards durable peace and prosperity and that of others because we cannot be helpful in everything and at every time. For the people with that attitude in the African Great Lakes Region (AGLR), a change of mentality is needed on this point. People need to be honest, humble, and original in everything they do.

- **Misconception or Misunderstanding of 'Providence', Too Much Focus on Past Events or history, and Negative Conception of Sense of Eternity**

The people with time mismanagement mentality (TMM) spend much time talking about the past events or history rather than thinking of what they can do to have a good future. As we mention in the previous paragraph, those people blame without end the white Europeans who colonized Africa for the problems that they are suffering today. While colonialism have some responsibility for the state of Africa today, but African peoples need to know that they are the first responsible for their situation of their continent. It can be agreed that what European colonialists did to nations of African Great Lakes Region (AGLR) continue to have negative impact of the lives of millions of people in the region today; but as long as the European colonialists are no longer present in the region doing colonization as before, the population of AGLR need to cure themselves the wounds that colonialism created in them.

We need to uproot any plant of conflict that has been growing there since colonial era. We need to change our minds and destroy all the seeds of conflict that have been put there by the colonialists; and many have been passing them from one generation to the other. We need to look to the future that is full of many opportunities to build our communities, our countries. It is time for Africa to stand up. It is time for Africa to grow up. It is time for Africa to look at a propitious future. Why? The main reason is that some countries have realized more than 50 years of independence but almost nothing has been done by post-colonial African political leaders to put their countries on the path of durable peace and prosperity for all.

For example, the alarming socioeconomic situation of the DRC is so eloquent to illustrate that. Other examples can be found in some of what is reported concerning Africa continent. Africa is said to be in need of almost everything – infrastructure, education, health care, consumer goods, and retail – making this continent a huge market opportunity that will reach 50 percent of people living in cities 2030. The African continent is increasingly stable with reduction of political coups and of debt and inflation; it will soon have the world's largest workforce that will swell by 163 million in this decade, by 2035 will be bigger than Chine's, and by 2050 it will have 25 percent of the world's workers.

The African continent is experiencing mobile exploding with the industry that employed 3.6 million full-time workers; the intra-African trade is in its infancy with only 11 percent of African's trade taking place within its own borders and this the lowest of any region of the world; in Africa, 20 percent of government spending goes to education which is the crucial factor that determine whether the rapidly expanding workforce is a boon or a bane; and the African continent contains most of the world's uncultivated arable land – having 60 percent of the world's potential farmland, this continent could become an agricultural powerhouse – and rich in oil and gas (Berman, 2013).

So, what is the problem? For example, if Uganda, one of the countries African Great Lake Region (AGLR), is said to be able to generate USD 40 billion in foreign investment on oil and gas and they never use time and means properly to generate an important sum of money to lead the nation's economy toward financial prosperity, that means there is a problem! A real problem that needs concrete solution! How then a country with such potential can be reported to invest time in plunder and killings in a neighboring country? What kind of leadership is that? What name can we give it?

It is time for Africa; it is time to have good leaders who do not look back in the history to waste time. It is time for Africa to have good leaders who know the right things to do at the right time, and for the right purpose. While we cannot be like westerners and are not supposed to be like them, we need not only to love what they produce (like industrial products) but also how they produce them with much attention on how they properly use their time to make products that can compete at the global markets in today's world. It is possible to learn from others althgouth you cannot do the same way they are doing. The AGLR should do that. Otherwise, Africa especially the African Great Lakes Region (AGLR) will always be 'consumer' of products manufactured by the West while we also need to be manufacturers of things that may competitively sell on the international markets instead of being only sellers of natural resources on which the buyers fix themselves the prices!

How can we envy and frequently use what other nations are making without imitating the way they do to achieve their goals to produce things? Do they have time mismanagement mentality and be creative or productive? A comparison between Western industrial production and that of African sound to be parallel to the comparison between Western and African concepts of time. Let's have a look at Western time compared to African time and judge the result with consideration to how the two parts of the worlds' economic disparities.

To Westerners, time is a set of stripes drawn on the tarmac that is on the road on which they drive at exactly constant speed, so they think they know exactly when they will cross these stripes. Westerners feel sure the road is straight, regular, and goes on forever. Unlike the Africans, their journey stops when they die, but dying soon is not a real possibility to most of them. European cultural superstition is that time runs regularly, and the future points in time come near in the same regular speed as past points in time withdraw. For westerners, the focus is on the now – and forwards towards what is anticipated to come – the	Africans have no such unshakable belief in the future. Constant speed over regular tarmac might be possible, but the car might as well break down, floods could take the road, and a relative might be met. Africans do not speculate about the future there are too many uncertainties. The chance of it being what we expect is considered low. Africans traditionally rely on emotional marks of time, like when you were born, when you married, when you had you first child, when there was a war. But as far as the future is concerned these marks are still to be made, and the African typically considers

future. For Africans, time flows from the present back into the past.	his or her influence on that as small. Africans have no concept of historical progress: in every life of every person the same happens. The past is a chain of events, places that are marked in memory.
For Westerners, a mechanical and numerical process requiring a calibrated and uniform standard of measurement. Years and months are based on natural phenomena – but these weren't precise. There was a progression from Sundials and hourglasses to digital clocks and milliseconds. But Because "Time is money" – business demands time must flow at a constant speed for everyone. Trains have to run on time and all of life is ordered around schedules and time. In reality, we experience a sense that time moves for us personally at different speeds, depending upon our activity and emotional state.	Africans don't care about preciseness or uniformity. Does the rain come always at the same time? Of course not. Does it come at the same time for all tribes? Certainly not. Why be more precise than the rain? African time is connected to nature, just as Western time, but the natural processes and events chosen to relate to are the ones emotionally relevant to African life. But not as a historical process. The African interpretation of time starts thus: events occur in some order: there is "before" and there is "after". In African languages, there is a number of tenses that indicate roughly "how much" before, and how

	much after. Time is the oral narrative of the past.

For the Westerner, there is past, present and future. For the African, Zamani is the ordered sequence of the events that took place in the life of the world. Sasa is what is now, what are the needs now, and what to do now. Time and reality end now, the future is unreal. There is no future yet. It still is to be made by the interaction of all forces in the world. Once made, it belongs to zero.

Source: Eldrbary. (nd). A Comparision of the Western and African Concepts of Time. From a web page by Bert Hamminga. Retrieved on 28th October, 2015 from www.eldrbarry.net/ug/afrtime.pdf

Boredom, hurry and stress are good things to start from in explaining African time to Westerners. We have to compare the Western linear dead physical time line (with "past", "future" and a perfectly regularly moving "now") with the African "living time." (Sasa) "Count down" and "train" highlight that the Westerner has to "fit" his activities in a dead mathematical time framework, and if he does not succeed, he will end up with shortage or surplus of "time". "Ambush" and "Rain" both involve a waiting upon nature. The African "non-clock" types of waiting or hurrying do not involve internal conflicts causing stress.	
Waiting:	
A "Count down" is not so	"Ambush" This type of

well know in Africa, but very familiar in the West. Suppose some race will so start. Everybody is nervous. The bodies of participants are ready to do what is supposed to be done, but the clock requires a delay. The adrenaline has been released, it tells the body to go, but the mind watches the clock and says: no! That is a clear situation of stress. There are many more examples of "countdown."	waiting is traditionally well known in Africa. It falls under "living time". That means that not a mechanical clock, but live events like birds, and the behavior of the prey "measure" time. What your watch says is irrelevant. And it is classified as having a "tension", because it requires full concentration, at least readiness to full concentration at any moment.
"Train" refers to the situation, virtually unknown in Africa, that you finished what you were supposed to do, and ready to do the next thing, but this requires something that will only occur at a given point in dead mechanical clock time. So: you finished some job and you can go now, but have to wait for the train. You get bored. Boredom is an internal conflict of activity-wish coming up in a situation	"Rain" African countries have two rain-times a year and many crops grow, and produce seed only in rain time. So when the rains start, they start digging. So, they wait for rain. Obviously, clocks are irrelevant here. Rain is no train. Rain just comes when it comes and you do not have to "catch" it.. Rain is a gift from the living forces of nature. Further the spirits that send it might be offended by

were no possibility for activity is seen.	preparations in advance.
Hurrying:	
"Deadline" A dead mechanical date-time is agreed and set. The process is partitioned and scheduled. Sub-deadlines are determined. Of course problems occur. Parts of the process get behind schedule. Stress is all over. Without a clear deadline, in the West things usually do not get more relaxed. So without a deadline, the mode of operation becomes "Race", dead time saving directed activity. This Western addiction to dead mechanical time has, in the rise of industrial market society, been sunk so deeply in Western culture that even leisure is filled with dead time competitive games.	The basic African type of hurry is "Catch" (since that is what you can do with prey, booty and thieves). The main vital feature is again that in "catch" your watch (dead time) is fully irrelevant. "Catch" is a living time process. The process lives its own time. You are fully concentrated on the action, not aware of dead time. It ends once you catch, fail to catch, escape, or fail to escape. You should not try to subdue nature. You wait till nature gives you. And this "waiting"-attitude is, in Africa, generally rewarded by nature. In fact, having to work is considered a sign of disfavor with the powers and spirits.

Source: (Eldrbary, nd).

TIME ORIENTATION	EVENT ORIENTATION
1 .Concern for punctuality and amount of time expended	1 .Concern for details of the event, regardless of time required
2. Careful allocation of time to achieve the maximum within set limits	2. Exhaustive consideration of a problem until resolved
3. Tightly scheduled, goal-directed activities	3. A "let come what may" outlook not tied to any precise schedule
4. Rewards offered as incentives for efficient use of time	4. Stress on completing the event as a reward in itself
5. Emphasis on dates and history	5. Emphasis on present experience rather than the past or future
Illustration: American Culture	**Illustration: Uganda Culture**

Source: (Eldrbary, nd).

Adair and Allen (2004) suggest ten principles for time management that seem to be meaningful and may help to people to be more effective and efficient if applied in life. They talk about developing a personal sense of time, identify long-term goals, make medium-term goals, plan the day, make the best use of your best time, organize office work, manage meetings, delegate effectively, make use of committed time, and manage your heath. Looking at the suggested principles, we find out that the five first may be used by anyone in the African Great Lakes Region even those who do not work in offices; but for them to work well anyone who uses them should be first of all cleansed from the time mismanagement mentality because principles are part of skills or seeds and they cannot grow well in a bad soil!

According to Adair and Allen, to best develop a personal sense of time to consider it as one of your most precious resources and that it is not to be taken for granted; this is very important to consider when addressing the issue of time mismanagement in the African Great Lakes Region

(AGLR). People of the AGLR with time misstatement mentality should change; they have to learn to be exploiting time to enhance their life standards. That is one of the most important requirements for durable peace and prosperity for all in the AGLR.

7.2.9. Harmful African Traditional Mentality (HATM)

"Just because something is traditional is no reason to do it, of course." (Lemony Snicket).

What is 'Harmful African Traditional Mentality' (HATM)?

The harmful African traditional mentality is a habit that makes people perform acts that they believe normal with reference to their traditional customs, but that violate the human rights. Such acts impede personal and integral development of many people in African societies, in particular, the women.

Some Manifestations of the Harmful Traditional Mentality (HTM) in the African Great Lakes Region

- **Bride Price (originating from 'Dowry' as a traditional custom)**

In the African Great Lakes Region (AGLR), there is a traditional custom of giving a dowry when men need to get married. According to most of the cultures in the region, the bridegrooms or their families (parents for example) are required to give symbolic and honorific gifts to the parents of the brides as a sign of recognition and union between the two large families (the family of the bridegrooms and the family of the brides). While this traditional practice is not supposed to be assimilated to any 'business or commercial practice' or confused with any possible price put on the bride, many parents and guardians in the AGLR behave as business persons who seek profits when dealing with marriage unions.

In fact, people with harmful traditional mentality (HTM) in the AGLR consider the female human beings ready for marriage as serious business opportunities in which they can find a possibility of improving their financial situation. By the way, when a man becomes a candidate to contract a marriage, the family members of the bride with HTM make it a big deal by making discussions (one or two and sometimes more) so that they may get the amount of money or things they need in exchange with the bride.

This traditional harmful practice has been considered as a factor contributing to violence and gender inequality in the AGLR because of the people who misuse it due to their mentality of commercializing women. That is not so different from the famous 'human traffic' that constitutes a severe abuse of human rights. People of African Great Lakes Region (AGLR) with the HTM need to understand that what they are doing in the region is lamentably impeding durable peace and prosperity for all.

When people develop negative mentality using some of their cultural practices as a mean of justifying their acts, they seem to feel okay with what they are doing. But feeling okay with your acts does not mean doing the right things. It may also be said that many Africans debating with much strain the influence of some local and international NGOs on their cultures without looking deeply on the reasons why that is happening. They argue that the NGOs are putting too much pressure to eradicate some of their traditional practices that are considered as harmful while they have the right to enjoy the practices of their cultures to show their true identities instead of being forced to practice the western cultures in their daily living. With a sense of respect to freedom of expression that allows people to say what they believe, think, and want to, we need to be realistic when assessing the reasons why some people or organizations engage in a certain activity.

By observing deeply, how people live with reference to their true traditional cultural norms and practices in the African Great Lakes Region (AGLR), you can conclude that there is a certain modification or distortion. Some cultural norms and practices were already eradicated by the influence of the modern life, especially in towns and townships; but some are still lived but distorted in terms of their traditional original meaning. That may be one of the reasons why some NGOs, authors, or particular activists may talk, write, criticize,… even propagate against it with the aim of making a positive contribution to the society where the practices are taking place and to serve advocators of the human rights that are supposed to be universally known and respect by anyone.

One of the most interesting activities against the harmful traditional mentality (HTM) manifested in the bride price practice in Africa is the first international conference on bride price organized by a Ugandan women's rights and development agency MIFUMU (founded by Comic Relief since 1999) on 16th to 18th February, 2004 at Makerere University in Kampala-Uganda. The aim of that conference was to reduce or remove the significance of bride price which is considered as one of the means of making negative contribution to acts of violence and gender inequality that impedes the improvement the life quality of families and the respect of the rights of children in the countries where that practice is happening (Mifumi, 2004).

When you make a good observation of what is happening in the African Great Lakes Region (AGLR) concerning dowry giving today, in many cases, you can found out that there are long discussions not so different from price bargaining activities. And sometimes, these activities end up by creating conflicts between the two families in discussion or reaching a conclusion that will justify the desires of the parents or guardians of the bride (received the amount of money or other items that correspond to the bride price they will) so that they may traditionally and officially allow the marriage of their daughters to happen by pouring a blessing over both the bridegroom and the bride.

In case of disagreement, sometimes things turn apart and conflict or quarrels may take pace as you can see it in the following illustration. And in some occasions, in the villages, townships, or towns of the AGLR, some bridegroom with serious shortage of money or required item to pay for the bride decide to start living together without the consent and blessing of their parents or guardians. As one of the common social results, we may mention the less respect and social esteem that the new illegal and non-blessed couple will have comparing it to the blessed ones. This is called in some local language as 'Kurendeza, Kuherula, And most of time, some Christian churches excommunicate them. They become 'sinners' and cannot be allowed to take part in serious religious activities. With such mentality in the AGLR, are the parents, guardians, and church-leaders allowing young people to live in durable peace and prosperity in the communities?

However, efforts are being made to top the bride price abnormal phenomena in the African Great Lakes Region (AGLR) by some gender balance activists and organizations. But still, there is too much to do because it's not just fighting against the phenomena; we need to be able to involve every person who understands the importance of the establishment of the durable peace and prosperity for all in the battle against that social disease with the aim of convincing the people with harmful traditional mentality manifested in bride price to completely change their mentality. That is very important because many people in the AGLR are infected by the virus of that mentality and the contamination will continue to be effectively transmitted to new generations if we fail to evolve as many people as possible in our non-violent fight against that practice.

In Burundi for example, it is reported that some people think it is normal to call a woman, who is preparing to get married, a 'cow'. Andrewdasein talks about that by inscribing,

> "Calling the bride a "cow" is normal. Because of their place in traditional society, cows here were (are?) revered animals. In Burundian weddings, the bride's family usually gives a speech in which they point out that in exchange for the dowry, they promised to deliver the "cow", i.e. bride. Then they ask the groom's family to confirm they have made good on their promise. The groom's family asks the groom whether they have delivered the correct "cow." The groom looks at the bride and says yes, and the crowd cheers." (Andrewdasein, 2008).

- **The Son Preference Mentality**

This is a mentally that prefer having boy children and girls. And for many couples in the AGLR, there has been serious loss of peace due to that. Do girls not spend nine months in the wombs of women as boys? Are they not human beings that can help African countries to settle in durable peace and prosperity for all?

- **Forced early marriage for girls**

This is a practice that destroys the future of many girl children in the AGLR. Forcing them to get married before the age of majority as if they were only born for that.

- **Boys advised to prepare for marriage** in order to have children even if it's not their vocation.

- **Female genital mutilation**

This practice that is universally recognized as a human right violation consists of performing procedures that remove totally or partially the external female genitalia or injuring the female genital organs mostly by traditionalist circumcises for non-medical reasons, but as a result of transitional beliefs the famous one being that of reducing the sexual appetite of the women! Can this harmful traditional practice have any positive impact that can help them develop towards durable peace and prosperity for themselves and others? Are African women happy with that practice? Isn't a serious violation of human rights? Can people expect durable peace and prosperity with the minds bombarded and paralyzed by negative mentality that manifested itself in their harmful cultural traditional practices?

7.2.10. Gender Imbalance Mentality (GIM)

"Culture does not make people. People make culture. If it is true that the full humanity of women is not our culture, then we can and must make it our culture."
(Chimamanda Ngozi Adichie)

What is Gender Imbalance Mentality (GIM)?

In order to understand well the meaning of 'gender imbalance mentality' in this chapter, we need to evoke the basic meanings of some related concepts like 'Gender', 'Gender Roles', 'Gender Relations', and 'Gender Equality or Gender Balance' because none of these words may be used to mean what we want to explain in this section. In a paper written by the Ugandan Ministry of Finance, Planning and Economic Development (MFPED) about gender inequality, 'Gender' is said to refer to socially and culturally defined roles, attributes, and privileges of females and males. The paper mentions that there exist biological differences between women and men but different societies in the world interpret and engineer the innate (God-made) differences into a set of social expectations about behaviors, activities, rights, power, and resources they have (MFPED, 2006).

Gender Roles is the allocation of certain tasks mainly to women and others to men even if both may be able to do some. And what is more on this point is that the attributed tasks are differently evaluated and rewarded by the society. The gender roles are different from sex roles and are not universal but are socially constructed and change with time and situations (MFPED, 2006). This is very important to know in order to discover clearly what needs to be seriously addressed concerning people with 'gender imbalance mentality'. And Gender Relations are defined as the social relations between women and men that are constructed on the roles attributed to them by the society. The gender relations are expressed in different ways, places, and times (MFPED, 2006).

The other interesting concept that often makes the title of news in Africa concerning the relationship between women and men in the society is 'Gender Equality'. This concept that sounds embarrassing to some African men may be understood in three dimensions. I may mean "equality before and under the law; equality of opportunity in economic, political, social and other fields; and equality in dignity (internal worth) of the person between women and men." (MFPED, 2006).

The concept of 'Gender Equality' is also called 'Gender Balance'. It is what sometimes troubles some African men who traditionally, culturally, and socially know they are not equal to women. They are not flexible to try to understand that gender role may change with time and situations; they do not want to admit that. They consider any teaching, advice, or propaganda of gender equality as mere provocation and very dangerous to their existing social harmony! Maybe because they seem to be unwilling to understand its socioeconomic advantage in African societies.

Their mentality is completely opposed to any issue or viewpoint that tries to mean that women and men are different but equal. They may seem to take part in seminars and teachings about 'gender balance', even talk about it in public as if they were supporting the principles; but never apply them in their daily living because in their minds they don't believe in them. This is the 'gender imbalance mentality' for some African men. And for some African women, the same mentality exists. Some may seem to agree with the importance of gender balance in African societies and say to be ready to non-violently fight for that, but in their minds, they nurture different views that originate in their traditional and religious beliefs! That is 'gender imbalance mentality' some African women. It is time for positive change of mentality as one of the fundamentals for durable peace and prosperity in the African Great Lakes Region (AGLR).

It is known that many NGOs and State institutions have been talking to people about the importance of gender balance in the AGLR; but it might be that many who listen to them do not understand well or they understand but do not want to believe in what they hear. Please, try again to get true information about the deep meaning and importance of 'gender balance'. Dig deep so that you may believe because there is no one who can make you change your mentality.

While you are reading these sentences it could be good for you to agree with yourself that the AGLR need women who are empowered to help establish durable peace and prosperity for all. And this cannot be effective unless both women and men of the AGLR change the gender imbalance mentality that seems to be impossible to eradicate with teaching, counseling, and propaganda.

Africa is not anymore in the primitive era and never will be.

We have to accept the truth that time, space, technology, advancement of science, and globalization in our developing world may push a nation to modify their traditional gender roles and relations although some social attributions seem to remain universal like taking care of the babies in families is predominately for women and fighting for the protection of the country is mainly for men.

The people of AGLR with the gender imbalance mentality (GIM) need to change because the actual situation of the countries of the region about gender imbalance is critical and cannot allow the majority of the families to live in peace and prosperity. For what is seen and considered as gender imbalance acts of millions of people in the AGLR are just the results of what is unseen by human eyes and which is buried in the minds of many that we call 'gender imbalance mentality'. That is where the solution to gender imbalance is to start; not just by condemning what is happening with the aim of establishing gender balance in the AGLR communities.

Is it not unfair to reign over the women like 'bad kings' while these people are doing too much work for the community to meet some of its basic needs? The women of the African Great Lakes Region (AGLR) suffer so much for the survival of the millions of people in the communities of the region. That fact needs to be honestly recognized. We have to make a good observation of people's daily life in the AGLR to find out the crucial roles that women play there.

You are going to suffer the consequence of your unfair and violent behavior at home. You always beat me violently, but your own children will kill you today. You always teach the importance of non-violence in the family to the youth at school where you work as a teacher, but your daily life doesn't show good example of your teachings. You are sometimes invited to facilitate gender balance seminars, but you never show it in your every day actions at home! You should die so that we live in peace!!!

You, brutal and aggressive father! You have been making our mum to suffer physical and moral torture; and she is the one who have been working hard for us to grow up. You are irresponsible; you often spend your salary to buy alcoholic drinks and to please your concubines. You should die so that we live in peace!!!

For example, for millions of people to have food in the AGLR, women struggle to produce a big part of what is needed in the poor agricultural sectors of the countries of the region, mostly with traditional modes of production using hoes! In fact, it is reported that,

> "According to the UN's Food and Agriculture Organization (FAO), 73% of working women in the DRC are farmers, representing 50% of the country's agricultural workforce. Congolese women face additional barriers to men in accessing credit and owning land, despite playing such an important role; less than 1% of sub-Saharan African land is owned by women." (On The Ground, 2014).

What is reported by FAO about the women in DRC shows how much women continue to be victimized by social systems that appear to be unjust. It is astonishing and pity-provoking to see people who are working so hard to produce what we need to have almost no ownership of the land on which most of their energy is wasted. If what these women produce does not fully benefit them, then the situation they are living is not so different from colonization!

The role that women play in agriculture in the AGLR is so outstanding that no one can visit the region without noticing what they do; especially in the village settings. What the women do is well-known. Any man with the sense of justice who sits to think about the role of women in Africa can agree with me that combating 'gender balance' principles or initiatives is the proof of having a dark mind about the socioeconomic importance of it. By arguing like this, we are not trying to show that women should be considered more important than men, and they can do safe and successful alone.

We just want to make a point that aims to show that, considering the socioeconomic role that women play in the Africa, they are supposed to be considered "unequal to men" in the African societies, especially in terms of human rights. They are supposed to be given the same opportunity as men, especially in concerning education and professional jobs. The following passage also puts in evidence the socioeconomic importance of women.

> "The crucial role played by women in agriculture in Africa is well-documented. Evidence suggests that empowering female farmers and workers, economically as well as politically, can have a variety of positive impacts across the different levels of social and economic organization: enhancing women's decision-making power and control over assets within the household; strengthening democratic systems and equitable allocation of resources within producer organizations; and helping to raise productivity and improve quality." (On The Ground, 2014).

The crucial role played by women in Africa plus the growing and systematic gender balance propaganda and campaigns should not be misunderstood and misused by some women of the continent to grow rude and violent against men (their husbands for example) as you we see it in the following image.

Countries with many corrupt political actors with 'Gender Imbalance Mentality' (GIM) will never accept to make women fully enjoy the rights that most men have by voting and implementing laws that give them right to the equitable allocation of resources, equal educational opportunity, participation in decision-making, etc. Such political actors may seem to be working hard to make better the lives of women or they maybe fully involved in mobilizing people to consider gender equality, but if in their deep inner there is still GIM, the result will be the same; nothing can change in a country if its acting political leaders do not change.

You have been reigning over us for many years; we have been living like your slaves since long ago in Africa. The gender balance in Africa means the time for women to have power over men. Your time is over; it is our time now. The gender balance seminars are so benefic for us. You should put an end to your outrageous acts if not I will put an end to your life!!!

So, all political actors of the AGLR with good conscious and who agree with themselves to have 'gender imbalance mentality' (GIM), need to change because if they do, their followers will also change progressively. And that will lead to positive change their countries, with in a good family condition to welcome durable peace and prosperity initiatives. The fruits of durable peace and prosperity are delicious, unfortunately they cannot be harvested by people who did not plant their seeds and work for the good growth of their trees! Stubborn people do not enjoy those fruits; that is why positive change need to be effective for all.

People who do not accept to change seem to be ready to help those who appear to be sadist, and who have sowed the seeds of conflicts and poverty in the AGLR; those people seem to be working day and night to make them grown to produce disastrous or atrocious results – the kind of harvests they are happy to have. Some of those sowers of conflict and poverty seeds have been working hard to make sure civilians are deprived of their rights. OXFARM (2012, p.2) writes about them by putting,

> "Weak state authority, the illegal exploitation of mineral wealth, and the ease with which weapons enter the country has helped fuel cycles of violence, with women, men and children caught in the crossfire. Civilians in eastern DRC in particular have been targeted by armed militia. The long-term instability and insecurity has left virtually no industry and limited opportunities for education and jobs. This provides an economic incentive for many young men and boys to take up arms, although they are also often forcibly recruited. Despite the government approving a progressive sexual violence law in 2006 that includes a broad definition of sexual and gender-based violence, women and men are frequently subject to sexual violence. Women face many inequalities in the DRC. They play a very limited role in public life and constantly confront deep-seated attitudes and beliefs that perpetuate discrimination and gender-based violence."

Now, can we expect any good initiative supporting 'gender balance' from non-civic men who are working hard to violence even the rights of other men? The deep-seated attitudes and beliefs that perpetuate discrimination and gender-based violence in DRC as reported by OXFARM is nothing but the gender imbalance mentality that is deep in most people's minds and hearts making them unwilling to let women live with full enjoyment of their rights.

So, at the center of the gender violence lies certain realities explained by the fact that the men with that mental attitudes for women think about themselves to be strong leaders (and sometimes kings) in their families and societies, protectors of their families, and the main decision-makers at home and in their societies.

Strongly influenced by the traditional gender roles of their societies, men know that they have to follow their traditional teachings and cultures in which women knew very well that they could never have equal rights to men. "Women were expected to care for children, prepare food, run the household, and dig the fields. They were expected to be submissive, and not to take part in public life – leaving them vulnerable to many forms of gender-based violence, as well as denying their economic, social and political rights." (OXFARM, 2012, p.5).

It can be wise to married men in the AGLR to agree with their wives about the importance of gender balance and think of good ways of practicing it for the durable peace and prosperity of their family. They should not wait until the women are taught about gender balance by the streets, churches, NGOs, or any other institutions. Because that may sometimes happen with new family conflict that will be hard to deal with and will put the peace of the family and community in trouble. That has been happening in the AGLR.

Married men should accept to change their mentality and take new responsibility to address the gender balance issues to their wives before any other person may talk to them about it. This sounds to be very important because the people or organizations who advocate for gender balance in Africa seem to have no intention of destroying the existing family harmony, but they just want to improve it to become more productive when the women are associated in some important issues like decision-making process, owner of income generating activity, etc.

In the DRC, it was reported that,

"The conflict has, however, significantly changed these traditional gender roles. Women report that taking part in the various committees set up by NGOs has given them the opportunity to participate in decision-making in their households and communities. Displacement towards urban and peri-urban centers and nearer main roads, introduced new ideas to men and women in previously relatively isolated communities. Perhaps more significantly, as men and women adopt new survival strategies, some women have started to play a more leading role in the family and community." (OXFARM, 2012, p.5).

Men should not seem to be revolted by women when they talk about gender balance. My humble point of view is that people should not be like they are accusing each other. The female human beings in the African Great Lakes Region should not be saying that the men have made them live miserable lives of injustice by discriminating over them since long ago. They should not consider all male human beings human right violators.

Even those women who have been violated by some criminal men in rebel armed groups should have positive attitude about men. The main reason is that when you look at how people come into this world you will conclude that women cannot exist without men because even science proves that they are the ones that determine the sex people. And men will not have effective existence without women... Marie Man and woman should accept that they are one as God intended it to be. And women in the AGLR should not try to show in the public that the minds of African men are stubborn because everybody can change for good or bad, and only God cannot change.

Although raped or kidnapped to save as sexual slaves, women in the AGLR should stop to be complainers by trying to be agents of change. OXFARM (2012, p.5) writes,

> "In narratives of sexual violence in the DRC, women have been simplistically presented as 'victims' and men as 'criminals' or perpetrators of abuse. This has overlooked the fact that men are also subject to sexual and other violence, and denied other roles for women besides 'victimhood'. These portrayals have had a negative impact on community dynamics, creating conflict and hostile relations between some men and women, and reinforcing the idea of militarized masculinity and other gender stereotypes that perpetuate inequality." (OXFARM, 2012, p.5).

The raped or kidnapped women may think they are the only victims of such acts; but even the men who did that had victimized themselves ignorantly! How is that possible? Those people cannot boast themselves in public about what they have done to receive praise! They are not moving safely; they are in permanent insecurity because of the wrong they have done! They have no peace of mind; they are tormented because of their dirty minds!

Those people can be brought to trial by a future serious and just government if they are identified! Etc. So, are the raped and kidnapped the only victims? That is why male human beings in the African Great Lakes Region should be flexible and ready to teach female human beings about gender equality so that they may be morally strengthened to be ready to help in the establishment of durable peace and prosperity for all even if they have the feeling of being victims since so long ago. Our regional nations need to understand that when men try to make women victims, both become victims.

Apart from DRC where the law 'Family Code' (Code de la Famille) is still discriminating against women, other countries of the AGLR have made great strides in creating laws for gender balance. For example, Burundi has adopted at the national level different strategies that aim to put an end to the existing inequalities between men and women. The national Constitution of Burundi voted in

March 2005 acknowledges the Convention on the Elimination of All Forms of Discrimination Against Women (CEDAW) as an integral part; and the noncompliance with that Convention means the violation of the National Constitution (Republic of Burundi & Easter African Community, 2009).

The article 22 of the Constitution of Burundi states that no one may be subject to discrimination based on their gender, origin, ethnicity, race, language, color, religion, philosophical or political beliefs, social status, physical or mental handicap, or suffering from HIV or any other incurable illness (Constitute Project, 2012 – Constitution of Burundi 2005).

Some Consequences of Gender Imbalance Mentality in AGLR and their Forms their Manifestation

The gender imbalance mentality manifests in different negative forms that make durable peace and prosperity for all impossible in the communities of the Great Lakes Region of Africa. People with such mentality fail to adequately use the potentials that are buried in other people's brains only because they have different genders (mostly famine). The most common forms of manifestation of gender imbalance in the AGLR are the discrimination of women by men, the discrimination of women by 'themselves', the family violence mostly because of Husband behaving as an 'outrageous king'.

- **Discrimination against Women**

The discrimination of women by men in most African countries, particularly in the African Great Lakes Region, has perilous consequences on the lives of millions of people. Many may seem to disagree about this reality but a deep and careful observation how women are treated in the AGLR will harvest several facts that constitute barriers to durable peace and prosperity for all in the region. Discrimination against women may result in the following realities.

- **Poverty**

It is regrettable to see the 'ingratitude' of some men in Africa who continue to treat women like objects they can use only when there are some needs to meet. This appears to be the mindsets of millions of men in the African Great Lakes Region; they abuse the human rights of women as if that is very normal. They don't consider women as having equal rights as men. That is one of the possible reasons why women are living in lamentable poverty in Africa – particularity in the Great Lakes Region of Africa – with sometimes no hope for the future!

Amadi and Amadi (2014, p.22) writes "According to the African Union 2004 policy document; The Road to Gender Equality in Africa; 'African women bear a disproportionate burden of poverty compared to men, a phenomenon that has been described as the 'feminization of poverty" Efforts have been made by many non-governmental organizations (NGOs), by some governments, by African Union (AU), and by United Nations (UN) but the situation seems to remain the same. Texts have been put in place serving as laws to ensure the rights of women, but their lives do not improve! Why?

The possible reason is that no one is there to respect the laws that guarantee the rights of women and no one is there to make them be respected. Why this situation? People's minds are still locked by old-fashioned and false views about women that may be summarized like this: they are weak and inferior creatures. That is the foundation of the gender imbalance mentality that is impeding durable peace and prosperity for all.

Laws and policies may change to make better the lives of women in Africa, but as long as many African men are still having gender imbalance mentality the situation will remain the same. We need to address this issue honestly and with all our energy because women are of great importance for the prosperity of our African communities. It seems that no society can claim to be 'peaceful and developed' when the majority of women are starving with poverty. Everybody in the African Great Lakes Region should be concerned about this issue, mostly those who are in leadership positions.

In Africa and mostly in the African Great Lakes Region (AGLR), women should be treated fairly if we need durable peace and prosperity for all – they should be as fortunate as men – and must be able to work to be productive to avoid poverty. Why? Here are some vital reasons for that:

- in the AGLR, women are the ones who generally give the first education to children; after giving birth, their children nurtured by their breasts;

- almost all the populations of the AGLR have been given first care and education women – they work so hard to make their children grow up unfortunately the males children pay back 'discrimination' to loving 'child-care' they have received from them;

- women, by and large, use their income to support the lives of their children while men most of them think about having a second woman or a concubine, enjoying life by posing egoistic acts such as personal nice food in a restaurant or bar, alcoholic drunkenness, etc. all those acts are unhealthy to the durable peace and prosperity of their families.

- etc.

These are just some of the examples that may justify why African women need to boost up their economic capacity because poverty is the enemy of durable peace. So, African men should understand that the durable peace that many are seeking cannot be possible when the majority of African women dwell in poverty. In poverty, they are likely to produce (give birth) and bring up children who will not become good citizens and that is a dangerous threat to the durable peace and prosperity for all in the AGLR.

- **Sexual Exploitation**

Now, the majority of women in the African Great Lakes Region (AGLR) are too poor to live an autonomous life. What can they do to survive? Some accepted willingly to be used sexually in order to get the minimum they need to survive. Some are taken by force to serve as sexual slaves! And what is the result of that? The most harmful consequence of sexual exploitation of women the 'trauma' that they experience and that unfortunately lasts almost all their lives!

The sexually transmitted diseases like HIV are the possible results of sexual exploitation that kill the inner peace and well-being of the women in the AGLR. Amadi and Amadi (2014, p.22) puts, "Force sex con contribute to HIV transmission due to tears and lacerations resulting from the use of force. Women, who fear or experience violence, lack the power to ask their partners to use condoms or refuse unprotected sex."

This reality cannot be a stranger one in the DRC, Rwanda, Uganda, and Burundi where fire-guns and other types of destructive instruments have been circulating illicitly. Most of the people in rebel armed movements have not been kind to civilians; some raped women and then kill their husbands and children – some have raped women and killed them after their inhuman acts – and some have taken women in hostage to serve as sexual slave. The following drawing tries to give us the picture of what has been happening in some part of the African Great Lake Region.

This fat woman is difficult to rape, guys! She is strongly resisting... You, if you don't want, you will suffer the consequence.
It is useless for her to resist. Willing or not, we are all going to penetrate by force. Let me start if you are failing to neutralize her power. I am sexually very ready!
No, please. I cannot be ready for such act. I already have three children resulting from rapes! They don't know their fathers. And the last rape infected me with HIV virus! No, please. Don't increase my suffering – don't give a fourth child – don't give me a new disease. Enough is enough. No, please.

Oh, Poor Raped Woman of the AGLR!

You are being raped by nonsense people, and after their acts, they take you to serve as their sexual slave. When the world learns about what happened to you, some feel sorry for you, but they do nothing to defend you. Both your psychological torture and psychical suffering will have an end one day. Those violent and nonsense destroyers will one day be eradicated in your country, and durable peace and prosperity for all will come home. That will be the work of some people of your own country that will be strengthened and protected by the Almighty God of peace to restore what have been destroyed by criminal gun-holders and plunders since the colonial era up to nowadays.

Don't lose hope, the time is near for true revolutionary political leaders in your country!

● Health Problems

Some sick women are victims of gender inequality in the African Great Lakes Region (AGLR). Because of being too poverty due to lack of the abuse of their rights (for example, right to inherit property, right to participate in the decision-making processes, right to equal opportunities as men, etc.), some women are suffering from some illnesses that have made them more and more vulnerable.

For example, many women in the AGLR have been victims of HIV/AIDS as a result of their weak social considerations; they are ill not because of their ignorance or personal will, but because the gender imbalance mentality that some men use to make them suffer. Amadi & Amadi (2014, p. 21-22) means the same in their article by putting "HIV/AIDS have been critical indicators of gender inequality. According to the (2008) WHO and UNAIDS, global estimates, women comprise 50% of people living with HIV. In sub-Sahara Africa, women constitute 60% of people living with HIV."

Moreover, generally in the AGLR, women are more exposed to diseases than men. They suffer from different types of diseases because of the gender imbalance mentality that prevails in many people's minds. In Uganda, for example, within Households, women were more likely to fall sick compared to men. However, women received disproportionately less treatment when sick compared to men (Ministry of Finance, Planning, and Economic Development – MFPED, 2006).

Mostly, this happens because women are economically weaker compared to men as a result of gender inequality.

Is this not an unfair situation? People who work hard to make sure the children in the families grow safe and healthy are the ones that are living very risky lives in the AGLR. Can we expect durable peace and prosperity for all with the gender imbalance mentality? Have a look at the following drawing at the next page and see an illustration of a woman carrying another woman towards the health center.

That is just one example of how some married women suffer from heavy duties, and remain without help or assistance from their husband; while it is surprising in other places of the world to see such scenes happening, this is still a reality in some settings of the AGLR where men with gender imbalance mentality strongly believe that it is normal and fair to treat women that way.

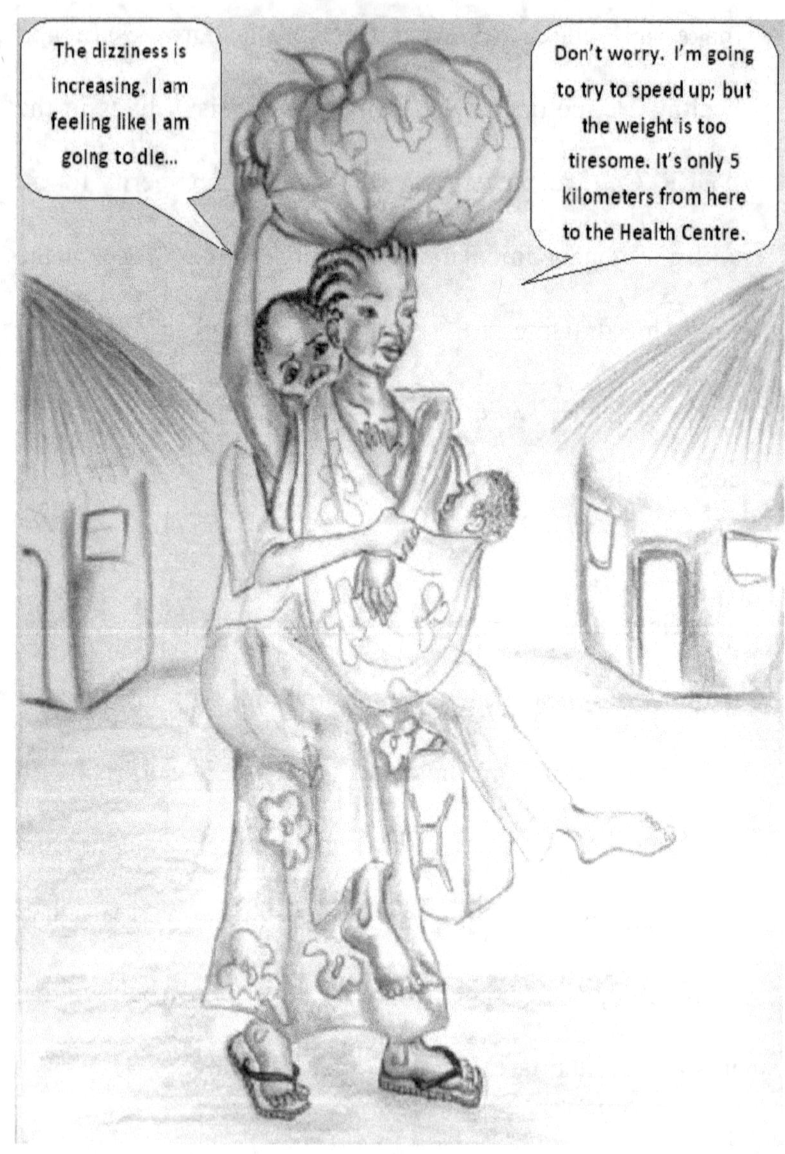
The dizziness is increasing. I am feeling like I am going to die...
Don't worry. I'm going to try to speed up; but the weight is too tiresome. It's only 5 kilometers from here to the Health Centre.

- **Unequal Educational Opportunities**

In African Great Lakes Region (AGLR), there are laws that condemn gender inequality; but in the educational systems of all the four countries of the region, there are unequal educational opportunities between men and women. Burundi, Rwanda, and Uganda are members of the East African Community (EAC). And the EAC Treaty recognizes the existence of gender imbalance in the community and provides inputs for gender balance showing its importance for the community's sustainable development.

> "The East African Community Treaty acknowledges gender, which is defined as being «the role of women and men in society», as one of its basic principles at the same level as good governance, social justice, rule of law, accountability, equal opportunities, protection and promotion of human and peoples' rights. In its Chapter 22 under Articles 121 and 122, the Treaty acknowledges the important role played by women in socioeconomic development and in business. The Treaty therefore provides that gender mainstreaming in all areas and aspects of member

countries is significantly important for the community's sustainable development." (Republic of Burundi & Easter African Community, 2009, p.9)

That being the case, one cannot think of the AGLR as a place where men and women are not given equal opportunities in terms of formation education (schooling); because even the national laws of most of those countries advocate for gender balance.

For example, as we mentioned in the previous paragraph, the Convention on the Elimination of All Forms of Discrimination Against Women (CEDAW) is recognized by the National Constitution of Burundi. Also, the constitution of the Republic of Uganda articles 30 makes education for Ugandan Children a human right, and in article 34 children are entitled to basic education by the state and the parents (Muhwezi, 2003, p. 1).

And in Rwanda, the National Constitution is in favor of gender balance and the Vision 2020 of country puts,

> "In order to achieve gender equality and equity, Rwanda will continuously update and adapt its laws on gender. It will support education for all, eradicate all forms of discrimination, fight against poverty and practice a positive discrimination policy in favor of women. Gender will be integrated as a cross-cutting issue in all development policies and strategies." (International Business Publications, 2013).

It seems that only the DRC has no or few legal texts or initiatives that support the rights of women, especially when talking about equal educational opportunities. However, in all these countries (Burundi, Uganda, Rwanda, and DRC) there are unequal educational opportunities due to gender imbalance mentality.

About Burundi, Jackson (2000) writes that there have always been far fewer girls than boys in schools since the establishment of the education system. He inscribes that in

1930, when the Catholic Church was organizing the education, there were 14,700 boys in schools run by the priest, but less than 700 girls in schools run by the nuns; and the situation is still the same even nowadays in Burundi for the Ministry figures showed that 44% of pupils in primary school were girls, and school girls represented 30%, and the women university students were only 25% (Jackson, 2000, p. 28 – 29).

The same unequal education situation between men and women also prevails in Uganda. About this country, Muhwezi writes,

> "In 2001, female school enrollment as a percentage of total enrollment was 49 percent and 44 percent at the primary and secondary school levels respectively (Kikampikaho and Kwesiga, 2002). Female students form about 35 percent of those enrolled in tertiary institutions. The adult literacy rate for Ugandan females is at 57% while that of males is 78 %." (Muhwezi, 2003, p. 1)

USAID & Uganda report states that it is mentioned in the Uganda National Development Plan (NDP) that gender inequality has led to unequal distribution of resources, opportunities, and violations of human rights; and the NDP gives measures to be used to redress the situation. The report shows that the key challenge faced by Uganda is that while policies and plans are clearly articulated on paper, their implementation lacks coordination or is non-existent (USAID & Uganda, nd).

That is common for almost all the countries of the African Great Lakes Region (AGLR). It can then be argued that some figures or statistics produced by some NGOs or Governments should be carefully examined by taking into consideration the real situation of people in the concerned regions or countries. It can be thought-provoking to read some passages of reports like this.

"The situation of women in Uganda is not encouraging. Although Uganda scores 79th of 155 countries in the Gender-Related Development Index and 33rd of 134 countries in the Global Gender Gap Index, the situation of women in Uganda in certain respects belies these relatively positive rankings. The total fertility rate of 6.3 is one of the highest in the world, and especially among adolescent females (over 147 births per 1,000 for girls aged 15-19). And, contraceptive prevalence for women 15-49 is only at 23.7%. Regarding nutrition, according to the 2006 UDHS, 38% of children under 5 in Uganda are stunted, 16% are underweight and 6% are wasted. And 50% of women and 75% of children less than 5 years are anemic. In education, while enrollment rates in primary school are nearly equal for boys and girls, retention rates are 53% for boys and 42% for girls. And secondary enrollment is one half for boys and one third for girls." (USAID & Uganda, nd).

And Rwanda, the country of AGLR that seems to have made more effort in fighting against according to the figures produced by NGOs and the Rwandan State, does not have a good standard of gender balance that can help the country to fully develop to durable peace and prosperity for all. If women constitute the majority of men in the country and are still very feebly represented in higher educational settings, Rwanda has much to do to fight against gender imbalance mentality.

Randell and Fish (2008) write that Gender in Rwandan Institutions of Higher Education Findings from former analyses of gender and education at the primary and secondary levels in Rwanda point to a persistent gender imbalance in retention, transition, and completion rates. They mention that the persisting gender disparities in Rwanda shape the context of higher education by posing serious obstacles to girls' opportunities to enter the Universities of the country.

- **Discrimination of women by 'themselves'**

The other form of manifestation of gender imbalance mentality in the African Great Lake Region is the discrimination of 'women by women' or by 'themselves'. It may sound bizarre to argue that some women are taking part in their own discrimination in the AGLR; but it is a living reality that because of false information that women have about themselves, and the outrageous lies that some men tell about women result in negative stereotypes that paralyze any women efforts to be effective participative contribution to the development of their communities. Kelly (2013) puts it clear by inscribing,

> "I think that many girls in the DRC are brought up believing that their calling is to serve men (Women Thrive Worldwide), which gives communities the idea that women are subordinate to men. Many women in the DRC believe they are supposed to serve men in any capacity, which allows for an environment for gender and domestic violence to occur. I think that the many campaigns, leadership programs and education programs are trying to change that stereotype of women, but teachers and communities need to focus on empowerment. By empowering women, they are able to break out of stereotypical roles and fight for equality. I believe that by teaching students and communities about equality, it will lead to less gender violence throughout the DRC. By making communities more aware of the problem, community members will be able to work toward a solution." (Kelly, 2013).

This may sound embarrassing for some gender balance activists in the African. Some are working hard day and night to help women become as productive as men; some are funding projects that aim to educate African women to have 'equal' job opportunity to men; and some others are putting pressure on some male leaders to be fair in the treatment of women!

But what will be the outcome of all these tiresome initiatives if most of the people you are working for do not believe they can be 'equal' to men? Is not a waste of time and resources to advocate for gender equality while the majority of women in Africa strongly believe they are 'different and unequal to men' instead of believing to be 'different but equal'?   Everyone who wants African women to be equal to African men in terms of rights must not waste his or her time and resources doing putting pressure on men or doing gender equality propaganda.

The starting point is the mentality of African women themselves. They can change positively Africa if they accept to change their gender imbalance mentalities (GIMs). They can become very active and productive in the process of bringing home durable peace and prosperity for all if the majority of them change their GIMs. African women should stop to think they were created to be enslaved by men. If they believe to be 'helpers' according to the Christian biblical teaching, they should know that 'helpers' are not 'slavers' and they contribute so much to the work of the people they are helping. They are supposed to be stronger or as strong as the people they are helping; they should not be weak.

All good leaders will be happy to work with helpers who do not underestimate themselves and who are strong, well-educated, creative, participative, and productive. Why? The helpers are supposed to valuably replace the leaders in times of professional annual leave or when they are absent for some personal reasons! So, African women, are helpers? Check well your traditional beliefs and the meaning of that word in your religious teachings.

Africa needs women who correctly understand their true roles in African societies and committed to fulfill them; without that durable peace and prosperity for all will remain impossible. Women, remember that you are useful agents of procreation; you have the natural power to bear, to support, and to sustain life. And some of you are doing that for the good of millions of African.

It could be more constructive if you could take new steps towards a future full of peace and prosperity with a clear understanding of your true roles and potentiality and be ready to use them in harmony with men, but not in competition with them. Remember that African men are not your gods and do not exist to be your God; they are your equal and you should be comfortable to work with them with equal esteem and respect to help establish durable peace and prosperity for all that the populations of Africa need – mainly the African Great Lakes Region – to enjoy their rich natural resources.

By talking about positive change of mentality for African women considering the change of gender imbalance mentality, we are not asking them to turn against the men impolitely as if they were telling them 'You have made us your slaves for many years, now it's our time; you have to pay back, it is time for 'gender balance'. No, that is not the point in our argument. African women should continue to respect the men (not only African men) but not fearing them; because the respect of African women towards men is a good moral value that will continue to make them desirable by men, and that is the mother of harmony in families in search for peace.

- **Domestic or Family Violence (Husbands as Outrageous Kings in some African Families)**

This is another frequent form of manifestation of gender imbalance mentality (GIM) in Africa Great Lakes Region (AGLR). Sometimes, we see battles in families between husbands and their wives; and sometimes, children hitting their parents or vice-versa. Most of time, the family violence does not happen accidentally. Behind any possible reason given about that, there seem to be some reasons due to the gender roles of some family members, particularly the husbands. For example, it is said that

Domestic and Gender-based Violence (GBV) is common in Uganda and often accepted as the norm by both men and women; this was proved in a comparative study of seven African countries in which Uganda had the highest rate of women having been subject to GBV with 60 percent and of women experiencing the violence from their partners or husbands up to 62 percent (USAID & Uganda, nd).

There are good reasons for positive change of mentality for women and men of the African Great Lakes Region. People should change the gender imbalance mentality; we do not mean that people should accept gender balance. Gender balance cannot be enforced; it comes by itself in a society in which people have positively changed their negative mentalities because the change does benefit all and no one will be the loser. People will only lose what were stopping them from embarking the boat of durable peace and prosperity – it all about the things or beliefs that were making them appear ugly to the world scene.

In the DRC, domestic violence is not even addressed in the laws of the country. About domestic violence in the DRC, it has been reported that "Although there are no official statistics, domestic violence against women, including spousal rape, appears to be common, and domestic violence has high levels of social acceptance." (Social Institutions & Gender Index, nd, p.2).

As it is about Uganda, the 2007 Demographic and Health Surveys (DHS) in DRC asked women if a husband was justified in hitting his wife for one of five reasons and 76 percent responded affirmatively to at least one reason; and during the same survey, it was found that 63 percent of women in the DRC have experienced physical or sexual violence from their partner or spouse at some point in their life (Social Institutions & Gender Index, nd, p.2).

Should we advocate for gender balance in a community where some women know it is normal men (husbands) to hit them for some 'faults'? Governments can try to protect women again family violence but if their mentalities are still unchanged the results will remain the same. It is written about the DRC that "Although the government has been increasingly responsive, addressing women's physical integrity through legislation, the culture of violence perpetuated through the ongoing conflict has meant that violence against women continues to be pervasive." (Social Institutions & Gender Index, nd, p.3).

Nonetheless, it has been reported that another major concern about family violence due to gender imbalance mentality is rape. This situation is often perpetrated by the sexual partners of women who consider it as their customary right. For example, in Uganda, rape has also been a tactic and consequence of long-term conflict and displacement. Though armed conflict has largely been controlled, it resulted in countless victims of sexual assault, as well as internally displaced people that are especially vulnerable before being resettled in their traditional homes (USAID & Uganda, nd, p.5).

It is sad to learn about some of the atrocious acts committed by men with extreme gender imbalance mentality in the African Great Lakes Region (AGLR). Women are not properties; they are human beings with rights that should be respected by others in the societies.

Should women be raped and later on be violently abused by the rappers that they should not deliver the pregnancy they carry?

What kind of minds do some rappers have? Is it not more dangerous than any other diseases? Should that kind of men behave in a different way and stay safe? Can you imagine a situation in which a husband violates the rights of his wife thinking that he has the right of doing anything he wants to her? Men of African Great Lakes Region (AGLR) need to understand at which level of economic development their countries are, and why gender imbalance mentality (GIM) should be considered as one of the main causes of underdevelopment.

References

Adair, J. & Allen, M. (2004). Time management personal development. The Concise. London: Thorogood Publishing Ltd

Africa Progress Panel (nd). Press Release – Plunder of Timber and Fisheries in Holding Africa Back – Kifi Annan. retrieved on 22 September 2015 from http://app-cdn.acwupload.co.uk/wp-content/uploads/2014/05/Press-release-ENGLISH.pdf

Amadi, L. & Amadi, C. (2014). Towards Institutionalizing Gender Equality in Africa: How effective are the global gender summits and convention? A critique. In African Journal of Political Science and International Relations vol. 9(1), pp. 12 – 26, January 2015. Academic Journals – http://www.academicjournals.org/AJPSIR

Andrewdasein. (2008). 6 ways Burundi is a little different. Retrieved on 9th November, 2015 from http://www.quakerfront.com/2008/06/08/6differences/

Anthony, K. I. OSA. (2015). J. S. Mbiti's African Concept of Time and the Problem of Development - International Conference on Humanities, Literature and Management (ICHLM'15) Jan. 9-10, 2015 Dubai (UAE) Retrieved from http://icehm.org/siteadmin/upload/2861ED0115034.pdf

Berman, J. (2013). Seven Reasons Why Africa's Time is Now. In Harvard Business Review October 2013. USA: Harvard Business School Publishing Corporation. Retrieved on 20th October 2013 from http://www.afriscope.com/fileuploads/Seven%20reasons%20why%20Africa%27s%20time%20is%20now.pdf

Bob, P. (2003). Purpose, Vision, Goals. Do you have a definite purpose that guides your ambitions, vision, and goals? Retrieved on 28th October, 2015 from www.askbobproctor.com/PurposeVisionGoals.pdf

Bob, P. (nd). Purpose, Vision, Goals. Retrieved on 28 October, 2015 from www.files.meetup.com/542315/Purpose,_Vision,_Goals_Lesson.pdt

Bussien, N. at al. (2011). New Issues in Refugee Research. Research Paper No. 197. Breaking the Spell: Responding to Witchcraft Accusations Against Children. Geneva 2 Switzerland: UNHCR

Challender, C. at al. (2003). Lifting the Resource Curse. Extractive industry, children and governance. Briefing Report. London: Save the Children

Cimpric, A. (2010). Children Accused of Witchcraft. An anthropological study of contemporary practices in Africa. Dakar: UNICEF WCARO.

Constitute Project (2012). Constitution of Burundi 2005. Retrieved from https://www.constituteproject.org/constitution/Burundi_2005.pdf

Crawford, A. (2012). Witnessing 'child witch' exorcism in the DR Congo. Retrieved from

Dilva, I.S.D. (2013). Africa's poverty persists as its natural resources looted, mismanaged. Retrieved on 22nd September 2015 from http://moonofthesouth.com/africas-poverty-persists-natural/

Eldrbary. (nd). A Comparision of the Western and African Concepts of Time. From a web page by Bert Hamminga. Retrieved on 28th October, 2015 from www.eldrbarry.net/ug/afrtime.pdf

Fade, J. D. (2013). The origins of African Society, from African History edited by Chima J. Korieh and Raphael Chijioke Njoku, p.47, Revised Edition, USA: Cognella, Inc.

Fagge, N. (2015). 'They accused me of killing and eating my grandmother': Agony of Congo's 50,000 'child witches' who are brutally exorcised to 'beat the devil out of them'. Retrieved from http://www.dailymail.co.uk/news/article-3276057/My-grandmother-died-said-witch-drink-salt-water-stuck-fingers-throat-pieces-said-d-eaten-Congo-s-child-witches-exorcised-devil-beaten-them.html

Fitzpatric, L. A. (2012). African Names and Naming practices: The Impact Slavery and European Domination had on the African Psyche, Identity and Protest. Thesis Presented in Partial Fulfillment of the Requirements for the Degree Master of Arts in the Graduate School of The Ohio State University. Ohio: Ohio State University

Free the Slaves & Open Square Foundation. (June 2011).

Slavery in Conflict Minerals. The Congo Report. Retrieved from www.freetheslaves.net

Gabriel, O. C. J. B. (2014). Department of Religion and Human Relations – Nnamdi Azikiwe University. 'The Transformation of "African Mentality" as Fundamental to the Development of African Societies' in American International Journal of Contemporary Research Vol. 4, No. 10; October 2014

Gardner, H. (2006). Five Minds for the Future. Boston, Massachussets: Harvard Business School Press

Hanson, K. & Ruggiero, R. (2013). Child Witchcraft Allegations and Human Rights. Belgium: European Union – European Parliament

Ian (3rd June 2012). Witchcraft and Poison in Rwanda. retrieved on 19th September 2015 http://ianinrwanda.blogspot.com/2012/06/witc hcraft-and-poison-in-rwanda.html

Igwe, L. (2011). A Conference on Witchcraft Branding, Spirit Possession and Safeguarding African Children. Retrieved from http://archive.randi.org/site/index.php/swift-blog/1521-a-conference-on-witchcraft-branding-spirit-posession-and-safeguarding-african-children.html

International Business Publications. (2013). Rwanda Business Law Handbook 1. Strategic

Jackson, T. (2000). Equal Access to Education. A peace imperative for Burundi. London: International Alert.

Jenkins, P. (2011). Laying Down the Sword. Why We Can't Ignore the Bible's Violent Verses. New York: Harper Collins Publishers

Keim, C. (2013). 'Changing our Minds about Africa', from African History edited by Chima J. Korieh and Raphael Chijioke Njoku, Revised Edition, 2013, USA: Cognella, Inc.

Kelly. (2013). Gender Inequality in the Democratic Republic of Congo. Retrieved on 10th October 2015 from https://conflictandemergencyzonesed.wordpress.com/2013/12/07/gender-inequality-in-the-democratic-republic-of-congo/

Kets De Vries, M. (2012). Are you a Victim of the Victim Syndrome? Faculty & Research Working Paper. INSEAD The Business School for the World. Retrieved from https://sites.insead.edu/facultyresearch/research/doc.cfm?did=50114

Kets de Vries, M.F.R. (2012) Are you a Victim of the Victim Syndrome? Faculty & Research Paper. France: INSEAD-The Business School for the World

Kombo, K. (2003). Witchcraft: A Living Vice In Africa in *Africa Journal of Evangelical Theology 22.1 2003, p.73 – 86*

Kombo, K. (2003). Witchcraft: A Living Vice in Africa. *Africa Journal of Evangelical Theology* 22.1 2003, p.73 – 86

Mail & Guarduans. 23 March 2009. Remains of Rwandan genocide victims 'used for witchcraft'. retrieved on 20th September 2015 from http://mg.co.za/article/2009-03-23-

remains-of-rwandan-genocide-victims-used-for-witchcraft

Mailey, J.R. (May 2015). The Anatomy of the Resource Curse: Predatory Investment in Africa's Extractive Industries. ACSS Special Report No. 3. Washington, D.C: Africa Center for Strategic Studies

Merriam-Webster's Dictionary and Thesaurus. (2006). Integrated Language Tools. USA: Merriam-Webster, Incorporated

MGLSD – UNICEF Uganda. (2015). Situation Analysis of Children in Uganda. Uganda: MGLSD & UNICEF.

Mifumi. (2004). International Conference on Bride Price 16th – 18th February, 2004 Held at Makerere University, Kampala, Uganda. Conference Report. Tororo – Uganda: Mifumi

Ministry of Finance, Planning and Economic Development (MFPED). (2006). Gender Inequality in Uganda: The status, causes and effects. Discussion Paper 11 August 2006. Kampala: MFPED.

Molina, A. J. (2005). The Invention of Child Witches in the Democratic Republic of Congo. Social cleansing, religious commerce and the difficulties of being a parent in an urban culture. Summary of the research and experiences of Save the Children's 2003-2005 programme funded by USAID. DR Congo: Save the Children.

Molina, G. A. (2005). The Invention of Child Witches in the Democratic Republic of Congo. Social cleansing, religious commerce and the difficulties of being a parent in an urban culture. Summary of the research and experiences of Save the Children's 2003-2005 programme funded by USAID. Retrieved from https://www.crin.org/en/docs/The_Invention_ of_Child_Witches.pdf

Muhwezi, D. K. (2003). Gender sensitive educational policy and practice: a Uganda case study. Background paper prepared for the Education for All Global Monitoring Report 2003/4 Gender and Education for All: The Leap to Equality. Uganda – Kampala: UNESCO.

Mwakikagile, G. (2006). Life Under Nyerere. Second Edition. Dar Es Salam & Pretoria: New Africa Press

Okeja, U. B. (2010). Witchcraft and Magic in African Context retrieved from http://www.inter-disciplinary.net/wpcontent/uploads/2010/02/o kejapaper.pdf

Okeneme, G. (2013). A Philosophical Evaluation of the Concept of African Freedom. In Open Journal of Philosophy 2013. Vol.3, No.1A, 161-167. Published Online February 2013 in SciRes (http://www.scirp.org/journal/ojpp)

Okpalike, C. J. B. G. (2014). The Transformation of "African Mentality" as Fundamental to the Development of African Societies. American International Journal of Contemporary Research Vol. 4, No. 10; October 2014 79. Retrieved from http://www.aijcrnet.com/journals/Vol_4_No_1 0_October_2014/10.pdf

On The Ground. (2014). Gender Equality – Project Congo. Retrieved on 10th October, 2015 from http://www.onthegroundglobal.org/genderequality/

Oniang'o, K, Ruth. Mutuku MSc, J. M., Malaba S. J. 2003. Contemporary African food habits and their nutritional and health implications. in Asia Pacific J Clin Nutr 2003; 12 (3): 231 – 236

Osborne, H. (2013). DR Congo's Witchcraft Epidemic: 50,000 Children Accused of Sorcery. Kevani Kanda's BBC documentary Branded a Witch uncovers horrific stories of child abuse in the name of fighting witchcraft. retrieved on 16th Sept. 2015 from http://www.ibtimes.co.uk/branded-witch-bbc-democratic-republic-congo-kindoki-469216

OXFARM. (2012). Gender Equality In Emergencies. Protecting Communities In The DRC. Understanding gender dynamics and empowering women and men, October 2012. Retrieved on 10th October, 2015 from http://www.oxfamblogs.org/eastafrica/wp-content/uploads/2010/09/cs-protecting-communities-drc-081012-en.pdf

Pan-African-Quotes. "Serve…Suffer…Sacrifice". Leadership and the Management of Change", Address by Mwalimu Julius K. Nyerere, Former President of Tanzania(1998). Retrieved on 28th September 2015 from https://panafricanquotes.wordpress.com/speeches/leadership-and-the-management-of-change-address-by-mwalimu-julius-k-nyerere-former-president-of-tanzania1998/

Randell, S. Dr. & Fish, J. Dr. (2008). Promoting the Retention of Women Faculty and Students in Higher Education: The Rwandan Case Paper presented at the Women's Worlds 2008 Conference 10th International Interdisciplinary Congress on Women, Madrid, July 2008. Rwanda provides a unique opportunity to investigate how public commitments. Retrieved on 15th October from www….. put the website here please.

Republic of Burundi & Easter African Community. (2009). Gender and Community Development Analysis in Burundi. January 2009. Arusha – Tanzania: EAC Secretariat

Ross, E. (2013). 'Impact of Christianity on Africa', from African History edited by Chima J. Korieh and Raphael Chijioke Njoku, Revised Edition, 2013, USA: Cognella, Inc.

SAFPI. (2013). Is there an African resource curse? Retrieved 23rd September 2015 from http//www.safpi.org/news/article/2013/there-african-resource-curse

Schermerhorn, J. R. Jr. (2007). *Exploring Management. Second Edition.* USA: John Wiley & Sons, Inc.

Senyoga, A. B. (2011) Witchcraft - a manifestation of poor work ethics. Retrieved from http://www.newtimes.co.rw/section/Printer/20 10-09-19/82587/

Senyonga, A. B. (September 19, 2011). Witchcraft – a manifestation of poor work ethics. Rwanda: The New Times Rwanda 2007 – 2015.

Social Institutions & Gender Index (SG). (nd). Democratic Republic of the Congo. Retrieved on 10th October, 2015 from http://genderindex.org/sites/default/files/datasheets/CD.pdf

Southgate, M. (2011). Rwandan Genocide: The Hutu Ten Commandments. Retrieved from http://passiontounderstand.blogspot.com/2011/08/rwandan-genocide-hutu-ten-commandments.html

Tierney, J. (1992). The Search for Adam and Eve. *Newsweek*. Retrieved from http://www.virginia.edu/woodson/courses/aas102%20(spring%2001)/articles/tierney.html

Tiernney, J. & Wright, L. & Springen, K. (2013). "The Search for Adam and Eve", from African History edited by Chima J. Korieh and Raphael Chijioke Njoku, Revised Edition. USA: Cognella, Inc

UNEP – MONUSCO – OSESG. (2015). Experts' background report on illegal exploitation and trade in natural resources benefiting organized criminal groups and recommendations on MONUSCO's role in fostering stability and peace in eastern DR Congo. Final report. April 15th 2015. Available at www.unep.org

UNEP. (2010). Uganda's Environment and Natural Resources: Enhancing Parliament's Oversight. Retrieved on 26th September 2015 from http://www.unep.org/publications/contents/pub_details_search.asp?ID=8194)

UNEP. (2011). Mon, Oct. 10, 2011. Retrieved on 25th September 2015 from http//www.unep.org/newscentre/Default.aspx? DocumentID=2656&ArticleID=8890.

United Nations Development Program (UNDP). (2015). Human Development Reports. Retrieved on 14th October, 2015 from http://hdr.undp.org/en/content/table-4-gender-inequality-index

USAID & Uganda. (nd). USAID/Uganda Gender Assessment. Kampala: USAID

USIP. (nd). Natural Resources, Conflict, and Conflict Resolution. A Study Guide Series on Peace and Conflict For Independent Learners and Classroom Instructors. Washington, D.C.: United States Institute of Peace.

Vlassenroot, K. & Raeymaekers, T. (2003). The Formation of New Political Complexes: Dynamics of Conflict in Ituri - Democratic Republic of Congo – Occasional Paper. Copenhagen: Centre of African Studies University of Copenhagen

Wofl, R. (nd). *Race and Racism. Illunimination Project Curriculum Materials.* Oregon: Portland Community College

World Bank. (2015). Burundi Country Overview. Retrieved on 25th September 2015 from http://www.worldbank.org/en/country/burundi/overview

World Bank. (2015). DRC Country Overview. Retrieved on 27 September 2015 from http://www.worldbank.org/en/country/drc/overview

World Bank. (2015). Rwanda Country Overview. Retrieved on 27 September 2015 from

http://www.worldbank.org/en/country/rwanda/
overview

Worldbank. (2013). Transforming Poverty to Prosperity
by Preserving Uganda's National Resources.
October 30, 2013. Kampala: Worldbank
Retrived on 26th September 2015 from
http://www.worldbank.org/en/news/feature/20
13/10/30/transforming-poverty-to-prosperity-
by-preserving-uganda-s-natural-resources